SHADOW OF SODOM

SHADOW OF SODOM

FACING THE FACTS OF HOMOSEXUALITY

PAUL D. MORRIS, Ph.D.

TYNDALE HOUSE PUBLISHERS, INC.
WHEATON, ILLINOIS

LIBRARY OF CONGRESS CATALOG CARD NUMBER 78–58510
ISBN 0–8423–5870–6, PAPER
COPYRIGHT © 1978 BY PAUL D. MORRIS
ALL RIGHTS RESERVED.
FIRST PRINTING, SEPTEMBER 1978
PRINTED IN THE UNITED STATES OF AMERICA

CONTENTS

PREFACE

Is homosexuality simply a creative alternative to the population explosion? Hardly. It is a symptom—not a condition—of a pathological state.

Homosexuals have now "come out," and they are making loud noises which are being heard. The hallmark of their message to the world and to themselves is captured in the words of the pastor and founder of the Metropolitan Community Churches of America, Troy Perry: "One thing is sure. We homosexuals must all learn to rid ourselves of the sense of shame that we have been conditioned to accept from the heterosexual world. Such shame is no longer acceptable to any of us. How could we go on being ashamed of something that God created. Yes, God created homosexuals and homosexuality."

Can this statement and claim simply stand unanswered? I think not. In these pages is an answer to the message of the Gay Liberation movement; an investigation of the pathology and etiology of homosexuality, and positive suggestions for the management of this very real sociological and individual problem. Also included are suggestions for positive heterosexual role influence on children, and ways to cope with a problem that confronts us on the streets, from video screens, and sometimes even in our own homes and churches. It is a look at what God has to say about the homosexual—and about the difficult calling of all Christians to mirror Christ's love to all mankind, homosexuals included.

Paul D. Morris, Ph.D.
Catalina Island, Calif.

CHAPTER ONE

DIMENSIONS OF THE PROBLEM

"My clients tell me that I'm a fantastic lay . . ."

The young man sat hunched up in the back seat of the cab, the soft glow of neon illuminating his gaze which played nervously with the raindrops on the window. His head was shaved, his expression sad. He was a homosexual prostitute.

Warning sirens screaming. Claghorns blasting. Cracks creeping along the bulwarks of present-day mores. With a mighty roar . . . the homosexual skeleton leaps from his closet into plain view.

It was not a surreptitious move. He did not tentatively arrange his dry-bone fingers around the edge of the door, timidly peek out, and then gently slip into the shadows unnoticed.

Like the Teton deluge, gay liberation is among us. He/She . . . it is rattling bones at our congressmen and President, tantalizing the tempers of the good citizens of Dade County, and insulting the integrity of Florida's sunshine girl.

Ed Davis, the former chief of the elite Los Angeles Police Department, was under intense pressure from a flood of protest generated by the gay community. The traditional pat-on-the-fanny has our gridiron gladiators worried.

Call out the National Guard! The Green Berets . . . but they too have been infiltrated.

The church!

The last bastion of religious and moral defense, surely she will help us? But, from that divine oracle comes these words: "Homosexuality is no more of a sin than short hair on women . . ." Or so says Dave Richards, a deacon in the Metropolitan Community Church, Los Angeles.

"Dave, are you really a Christian?"

"You bet I am!"

"How do you know?"

"Because Jesus died for me as much as he did for anyone."

"But are you absolutely certain you are going to heaven?"

"Absolutely!"

"Yes, but being a homosexual, how can you know that?"

"Because Jesus said I have eternal life and nobody can take it away from me."

"Yes, but . . ."

"See you there, pal."

OK. So just how large is this problem? How many homosexuals are there in America? What is their social and political strength? If we really believe that what the homosexual community is doing is wrong, how do we go about neutralizing its effect? Or should we try?

The attitude of the American Psychiatric Association was well defined when, on December 15, 1973, its trustees decided to drop homosexuality from the association's list of mental disorders. (A decision, by the way, with which this writer concurs.) When put to a vote among the entire membership of the association, only about 65 percent voted, and of that, 60 percent sustained the action of the trustees. The wording was then changed to categorize homosexuality as a "sexual disorientation disturbance." When viewed from another angle, 6,000 psychiatrists out of a total of a 17,000 membership have effected a change in the psychiatric bible, otherwise known as *The Diagnostic and Statistical Manual of Mental Disorders.*

One study has revealed that, of a well-educated higher middle class stratum of society, one out of every three males and one out of every five females had had homosexual experiences involving orgasm. Kinsey has estimated that 4 percent of all American males (four million plus) are *exclusively homosexual all of their sexual lives;* 8 percent (eight million plus) are exclusively homosexual for at least three years between the ages of sixteen and fifty-five, and that 37 percent of all American males have some homosexual experience after marriage. These statistics can be roughly cut in half for women. Bieber points out that of women who engage in homosexual relations, one third of them are exclusively homosexual. The incidence of exclusivity is higher, therefore, with females than with males.

Simply put, what all these statistics mean is that *over half* of our country's population either has had or will have some experience with homosexual relations before the age of fifty-five. It also means that 6 to 7 percent of our population is exclusively homosexual all of their sexual lives. To get some perspective on the size of this group, it is larger than half of the total number of black citizens in our country.

Out of this number has developed a sizable contingent of militants. By militant we do not mean politically or personally violent. Instead, it refers to a determinism and honesty among homosexuals that is causing them to declare themselves as a viable segment of society. This militancy reaches across the spectrum of the homosexual community and includes the far right (the evangelical gay church), as well as the far left (the most liberalized libertines).

San Francisco is the focus of this militancy. Indeed, San Francisco is the focus of the homosexual cause in the United States with Los Angeles and New York running some distance behind. The first *Gay Pride* parade was held in Los Angeles, organized and initiated by the Rev. Troy Perry, pastor of the first Metropolitan Community Church and founder of the subsequent denomination. He describes the parade in his book, *The Lord Is My Shepherd and He Knows I'm Gay:*

We couldn't get the bands we wanted to have, nor the horsemen, nor a lot of floats, but we did exceptionally well anyway. The parade started with Willie Smith driving his VW Microbus, and playing some recordings of World War II German marches over an amplification system he had hooked up. Right behind him was the Society of Anubis, a social group of the hinterlands. They owned a retreat house out in the San Bernardino Mountains. And here they were, militant conservatives, going down Hollywood Boulevard with a float and the goddess of Anubis on a white stallion.

The alphabetical order was a little haphazard. Behind the Anubis section was *The Advocate* float bedecked with a carload of groovy guys in bikini swim suits. This was a mass of muscle calculated to turn everyone on. It did. After the male beauties all fresh from their triumph at their annual contest, the parade ran the gamut of just about anything you could name. I think Focus was next. This is a pretty conservative gay group from the extremely conservative Orange County. The Focus group carried a large sign reading, "Homosexuals for Ronald Reagan." I heard one woman spectator on the sidewalk say, "I can forgive them for being homosexuals, but not for being for Ronald Reagan." Gay Liberation came marching down the street carrying banners and shouting, "Two, four, six, eight—gay is just as good as straight." That drew two kinds of comments from the sidewalk crowd. One was an enthusiastic echo, the other derision. But the marchers were followed by the chilling spectacle of a Gay Lib float with a young beautiful man fastened on a cross. Above him a large black and white banner was emblazoned with the words, "In Memory of Those Killed by the Pigs." Reaction to that was a silent shock wave that stunned and chilled all the spectators. To turn the mood back to the festive occasion, there was also a Gay Lib Guerrilla Theatre. This was a flock of shrieking drag queens [men dressed as women] all wearing gauzy pastel dresses, and running every which way to escape club wielding guys dressed as cops and sporting large badges with the word "Vice" splashed across them.

Another organization marching with us was a group of friends carrying a large sign reading, "Heterosexuals for Homosexual Freedom." It was a direct, welcome, and reassuring gesture. This is happening oftener, but we need a lot more of it.

A fife and drum accompanied the flag. There were drag queens. One section that particularly amused me was the pet section. Pets were carried, led, and pushed; some were in cages, some in highly decorated cases. Topping that off, one fellow had a big white husky dog on a leash. He had a sign on his dog reading, "All of us don't walk poodles." There was a motorcycle group in black leather led by a butch young man resplendent in black leather jacket, pants, gloves, and dripping with chains that seemed to encrust his heavy costume. To set this off in a frolicsome mood he wore pink high-heeled shoes.

Pat Rocco's group, SPREE (Society of Pat Rocco Enlightened Enthusiasts), had a large number of colorfully costumed people, many carrying SPREE signs and slogans about gay films. Several wildly decorated cars also carried SPREE girls and many handsome young men who had appeared in Pat's films. The whole SPREE group was preceded by an enormous lavender banner that spelled out the SPREE name. Rocco is a close personal friend of mine. He is also the leading film maker in the gay community.

Signs carried in the parade were slogans that we now see with increasing frequency. Here are some samples: "Homosexuality Is Natural Birth Control"; "More Deviation, Less Population"; "America: In God We Trust . . . Love It But Change It"; "Nazis Burned Jews, Churches Burned Homosexuals"; "Hickory, Dickory, Dock, They'll Pick Our Bedroom Lock, They'll Haul Us In and Call It Sin, Unless We Stop Their Clock."

We were the last in this smoothly run parade. I rode in an open convertible. Behind me came the congregation singing "Onward Christian Soldiers." We were gay, and we were proud.[1]

This was one of the first but by no means the last of such parades. Recently, in response to the "Save Our Children" campaign led by singer Anita Bryant and others, a parade was held in San Francisco which drew more than 300,000 plus 75,000 participants. It was an expression of Gay Pride that took nearly four hours to move up Market Street from the Embarcadero to City Hall.

David Johnston, *Los Angeles Times* staff writer, noted in a column that

. . . the crowd, more than double that at last year's parade, was the result of Anita Bryant's successful campaign to repeal a gay rights ordinance in Dade County, Florida.

In contrast to the party atmosphere of last year's parade—with its nudity, sexual activity and men hugging and kissing each other—this year's parade started off more like a protest march. As the participants marched they chanted numerous political slogans, including, "The People United Cannot Be Defeated," "Civil Rights Is Not the Solution, What We Need Is Revolution," and "Gay Teachers Fight Back."

Many of the floats, banners and signs attacked Miss Bryant. Some labeled her a hypocrite for being a Christian who "hates" homosexuals. Others cast explicit aspersions on her sexual proclivities. Both the parade participants and their signs represented virtually the entire range of sexual interests. There were men in women's clothing posing for photographers, women in men's clothing whom the photographers ignored, squads of men in black leather jackets and pants and one man in a black leather garter belt, nylon stockings, heavy leather boots, purple panties and nothing else.

There were signs championing "Dyke Power," "Lesbian Mothers' Rights," "Los Angeles Gay Teachers" and "Dyke and Faggot Anarchists." Several posters compared Miss Bryant to Adolf Hitler, Josef Stalin, Senator Joseph McCarthy and Idi Amin.

Don't make the mistake of thinking that this kind of militancy does not produce results. In San Francisco the sheriff and many other officials including the mayor could not be elected without homosexuals' support. Of a total population of 680,000, an estimated 120,000 are homosexuals, and officials reckon that 28 percent of the city's voters are homosexual (*Newsweek*, 6/6/77, p. 25).

In 1975, the San Francisco school board outlawed discrimination because of sexual orientation. The board went even further by voting 7 to 0 to revise the school system's family-life curriculum to acknowledge homosexual life-styles. Accordingly, education officials in San Francisco announced plans to introduce a new public school curriculum to "sensitize" students to accept—or at least tolerate—homosexual life-styles as just another way of living (*Christianity Today,* 7/8/77, p. 36).

The Media

"Some clergymen believe that this [homosexuality] is one of the toughest problems the church has had to face . . . more than women, more than black. . . ." The attractive television interviewer went on to explain more about the "problem," and introduced two opposing principals in the Dade County controversy and proceeded to interview them. The debate became heated and the interviewer became incidental to the exchange between the two opposing personalities. This "interview" took place on a popular network talk show and was viewed by millions. Such talk shows on both radio and television are immensely popular. Many give listeners or viewers the opportunity to "call in" and talk firsthand to the personalities. The subject of literally hundreds of these programs is homosexuality and homosexual human rights.

Almost daily in the *Los Angeles Times,* one can read an article or an editorial or a letter to the editor reporting or discussing the same basic subject matter. Probably no specific social phenomenon has received more media attention than homosexuality and its attendant milieu.

One may challenge this by raising the issues of hunger, highway carnage, welfare, crime, and war. Of these, only crime and warfare can legitimately challenge the networks and newspapers and magazines in competing for space with homosexuality. War, of course, is always preemptive. But it is, shall we say, *seasonal.* Crime is too general to be compared with a specific item like homosexuality. Anyway, much of crime finds its most ugly and grisly expression in the homosexual scenario.

While this is being written, the most extensive and

bizarre multiple murder incident in history is being investigated. You guessed it, those charged with the crime are self-confessed homosexuals. All of the victims were allegedly homosexuals. Much local and substantial national news space in all mass media is committed to this investigation.

To what extent is the problem influenced by all of this media attention? There is no way to be absolutely certain. One may say that reporting and dialogue which say positive and reinforcing things about homosexuality contribute to its spread and social acceptability. One may also argue that as long as balance is maintained, these arguments are neutralized . . . and the net result is no gain or loss. Certainly reporting concerned with the criminal aspects must act as a reinforcement to those stringently or even marginally opposed to homosexuality. Perhaps it even acts as a deterrent to those who would otherwise be susceptible to indulging.

Whatever the effect the media has upon the suppression or abetting of homosexuality, it is certain that the masses *are being exposed* to it in a manner unprecedented in history. It *is* bringing the issue of human rights for homosexuals before the nation for evaluation. The news reporting agencies might say this is not true, that the *newsmakers* are bringing it before the people. But do not forget that it is the agencies themselves that decide what is and is not newsworthy. And in spite of vehement denials, only the most naive could not detect bias in these decisions and in how it is presented to the public.

The Medical Community

Are there homosexual medical students and physicians? Unless medicine has some special characteristics which repel homosexually oriented applicants, there should be about 20,000 homosexuals in our profession.[2]

One estimate places 800 practicing homosexual physicians in New York City alone. However, do not panic! Even if your doctor is a homosexual, his competency is probably not influenced by it. There is something to be said for the case that a male homosexual urologist would not be any more interested in the penis of a patient than a male heterosexual gynecologist would be interested in the vulva of a female patient . . . unless said interest is clinical.

Homosexual doctors can be found in any specialty. Perhaps there are some homosexual doctors who are influenced by same sex nudity, but no more so than heterosexual doctors are with patients of the opposite sex. The fact is, that given conscientious professional competence, sexual orientation should not affect patient-physician relationships.

Should a homosexual *pediatrician* immediately be suspect? Does one worry about a heterosexual male pediatrician examining infant girls?

Dr. Henry D. Messer, a surgeon who is also a homosexual, offers us this explanation of himself:

After many years of studying the subject of homosexuality from an intellectual and scientific as well as from a personal aspect, I must conclude that I am an emotionally healthy and stable person, certainly no less so than most heterosexuals. I just prefer a different kind of sexual pleasure than most of the doctors you know. I think of homosexuality as akin to left-handedness. It is certainly an inconvenience, but not an illness.[3]

No doubt the number of homosexuals in medicine corresponds roughly in proportion to the number of homosexuals in the overall population. But it is not necessary to conclude, no matter what our moral or religious scruples, that these physicians are incompetent or a sexual threat to the patients under their care.

The Athletic Community

Sport, allows James Michener, is not necessarily a builder of character. In fact, it is at times, character destroying.[4] The fiction that athletics and sport are in some way exempt from the decadence of our society is widely held by many. Yet there is much in the sporting world which is anything but pristine. So it need not come as a shock to learn that some of our national athletic heroes are gay. Frankly, I do not know of any heroes who *are* gay. But my research has indicated that the reason for this is not so much that there aren't any, but that no one is going to come right out and say so without seriously damaging his economic, if not his social stability.

David Kopay, of the National Football League, far from being a superstar (which gives him some latitude in this regard), has openly admitted his homosexuality. He has written a book with Perry Deane Young entitled, *The David Kopay Story*. He is making the talk-show circuit promoting its sale, declaring that ". . . it's really been a high for me to get these things out in the open."

Kopay is described as having a hard-nosed reputation as a football player. This is to indicate that he is anything but effeminate and sissy. He was co-captain on Washington's 1964 Rose Bowl team. As a free agent he signed on with the San Francisco Forty-niners. He was traded to Detroit, then moved to Washington (where he played for the late Vince Lombardi) and New Orleans. His final association with pro football was with the Southern California Sun of the defunct World Football League. It was while he played for the Redskins that he learned he wasn't the only gay football player in the NFL.

A *Los Angeles Herald Examiner* staff writer has pointed out that Mr. Kopay could use a little compassion and understanding. After all, right now his life is at third and long yardage. And it's doubtful he'll punt.[5] The writer may be right. But when one takes a cold look at reality, one is prompted to remind Mr. Kopay that life, like football, is played by the rules, and if he doesn't punt, it's likely he'll be creamed in his own end zone.

The Military Community

Again, homosexuals in the military can be estimated in accordance with the proportion of the overall population. The attitude of the military toward homosexuals is definitive. The enlistment papers require everyone to answer the question, "Do you have, or have you ever had measles, mumps, scarlet fever, mental disease, homosexual tendencies . . . etc." Almost all homosexuals answer the question in the negative as it pertains to their gayness.

During the draft years, the question all but lost its meaning because many inductees would deliberately answer the question in the affirmative just to keep from being drafted. It didn't work. They were drafted anyway and processed through a routine psychiatric examination (in some cases) and plopped right back into duty. The Army reasoned, we surmise, that if their activity went undetected, there would be no problem. Some were discovered and given less than honorable discharges.

This section exists merely to call attention to the fact that homosexuality in the military is a serious problem. Broad information is available in the volume, *Homosexuals and the Military* (Colin J. Williams and Martin S. Weinberg, Harper & Row, Publishers, New York, 1971).

Homosexuality in Prisons

It had been seven hours since the handcuffs and the waist chains had been removed. The orientation procedure which provided the man with the information he would need for his new life in prison had been brief. He was now sitting on his bunk with his cell door open. Later that afternoon at four o'clock a count would take place and he would be locked in his cell until the following morning, when everyone would be permitted to go to the main mess for breakfast.

He was twenty-three years old and married to a lovely Christian girl whom he had met in high school. College was behind him and seminary was almost complete when he was arrested. While in school, he had served as youth and music minister at a nearby church. He was well liked, good looking, energetic, and constantly creating new ways for the kids to enjoy their relationship with the Lord and their church.

He had crossed the state line just as the flashing red light in the rear-view mirror caught his eye. Glancing at the speedometer, he realized that he had been exceeding the speed limit as he passed through a radar station. The officer was polite enough, informed him of his violation, asked for his license, and proceeded to write out a citation. Just as he was signing the notice to appear, the officer's partner approached the car with his gun drawn and pointing directly at him. He was rudely yanked from the car, twisted about, cuffed and accusingly informed that the car he was driving was reported stolen. It was news to him. He had borrowed the car while his was being repaired, with the intention of visiting a relative who was in the hospital in a neighboring state.

The officers searched the car and discovered a kilo of raw heroin in the trunk. The federal authorities were called in because he had crossed the state line. The evidence was incriminating. The judge sentenced him to three years in a federal minimum security correctional camp. There was not enough room in the camp facility to which he was sent, so the prison authorities simply transferred him inside to the medium-security buildings.

When the steel-barred door slammed shut behind him,

all hope of justice left him. He could not believe this was happening to him. He did not understand how the Lord could let this happen to him. He was guilty of nothing, but he was feeling devastating pangs of self-incrimination. He had let his family down—his wife and especially his Lord—or so he felt. Depression and anxiety hammered at him. There were no tears, no outbursts, no talking, no rationalization. Only numbness and fear. He needed to go to the bathroom.

Turning from the urinal, he had not yet zipped up his pants when he saw the black man behind him swinging a length of pipe. He just had time to raise his arm to fend off the blow when it struck. If the blow had hit him full force it could have killed him; as it was, his scalp split open and he fell to the floor dazed and bleeding. When his head cleared enough for him to realize what was happening, he became aware that the man was removing his pants. As more of a reflex action than a reasoned response, he lashed out with his foot. He found his mark. The man reeled back, hands clutching at his groin.

Not realizing his own strength or the extent of his injury, the young minister was instantly on his feet. Seizing the attacker by the head, he rushed toward a frosted window. He smashed the larger man's head through the glass, holding him in such a way that if he tried to extract himself, his neck would be sliced by the window's jagged edges. At that instant the young minister felt himself being pulled away by his fellow inmates. Blinded by his own blood, he sat down and began to cry.

His injury, while messy, was not serious. A couple of hours and eighteen stitches later, he was being interrogated by the captain of security and two guards. They wanted to know who had done this to him and if he would press charges. He knew who the man was but did not tell them. Somehow, his intuition told him that to tell on his attacker would be worse for him than if he remained quiet. His intuition was right.

Later, he was told that if he had squealed, he would have been killed by a "hit man" in the prison population. As a result of his not squealing, he was provided with two bodyguards—prisoners who volunteered to protect him from further assaults. In addition, his attacker came to him and apologized and promised never to bother him again. He spent his first night in prison with a terrible headache, but with the comforting knowledge that he had been accepted by the men with whom he would spend the next three years of his life.

If you did not know that you had walked into a maximum-security federal prison, you would think that you were sitting in the office of the pastor of a large church. The carpet was gold, the desk was large and expensively crafted, the sofa and chairs comfortable, and the decor and appointments tasteful. I was interviewing the protestant chaplain who had recently informed the parents of an inmate that their son had died in a knife fight that week.

The chaplain was clearly evangelical and had been describing to me the many exciting ways in which God had been demonstrating his power among the prison population. I was there representing Prison Fellowship, an organization started by Charles (Chuck) Colson of Watergate fame, and a few of his closest colleagues. We were discussing the effect of a recent seminar held at the prison, which was designed to generate spiritual growth and to introduce inmates to Jesus Christ.

All the time we talked, this book was in my mind. I wanted to ask the chaplain what he knew about the infamous reputation of homosexuality in prisons. When at last I began to question him about it, his answer startled me. "Well," he responded, "if you're young and good-looking the bottom line is *always* this: It's either fight or be raped."

During research for this section of the book, I interviewed a number of inmates—including the one whose story appears in the opening lines—some put their thoughts on paper. Here is one of them . . .

I have seen quite a bit in my seventy-five months of incarceration. The general outlook on homosexuality within prison is one of indifference. Most inmates allow it to exist with the attitude of, "He can do his thing as long as it doesn't interfere with mine."

Homosexuality is a major source of concern with the administration of any prison. The dominant homosexuals will occasionally fight and kill for the "favors" of the passive homosexual. "Dominant" far exceeds "passive" in numbers.

There are three categories of homosexuals in prison. One who indulged before he entered prison is a homosexual. "Jailhouse punk" is one who is pressured by others, engages through fear, or to merely satisfy sexual desires while locked up. He is taken advantage of anywhere, anytime. "Commissary punk" is the guy who does it for pay. He may or may not have a "pimp."

The "jailhouse punk" has usually led a very sheltered life and often comes from a wealthy family. Crime was a last resort for most of them; or maybe just something to kill the boredom. Whenever prison officials become aware of such a "punk" situation, either by the individual being forced or by an informer, they take steps to remove him from the population for his own protection, and then they remove the one who started the problem. These, if they are known, are brought to trial for sodomy and rape if the guy is hurt and willing to testify. The problem is that few are willing to accuse their tormentors because they will be labeled as a "snitch," or a "rat." And that is worse—much worse—than being called a "jailhouse punk." Fear is the motivation; fear of death or being hurt. In this instance only the one forced to practice the homosexual act is hurt. He is not fought over, no riot will occur. He is considered community property and anyone can have him.

The "commissary punk" was probably a homosexual

on the streets. Cigarettes, coffee, or drugs are his price. Anywhere from $10 to $50. He will make enough in a day's time to supply himself, his pimp, and friends with enough drugs to feed their habit.

From this group comes the violence and riots. It will start with some guy wanting sex who has no form of payment. He will promise—usually more than the homosexual asks. He will paint pictures of large drug shipments coming in. The homosexual will agree to the credit deal. For weeks the homosexual will ask for his money and the guy will continue to mislead him until finally he says that the drug deal fell through. If the homosexual has a pimp, the pimp will then reason that he must hurt, or kill the guy, because if one gets away with it others will think they can too. This line of reasoning easily builds to riot proportions. "Commissary punks" live in a world of fantasy, lies, and fabrications. They spin pretty tales of possible sex changes with all the money they will make selling their body. They dream of big houses, on big hills, with bigger orgies running night and day.

Finally comes the homosexual. He is usually very feminine in his demeanor, his walking, dress, and conversation. They prefer to be addressed by a female name and called "girls." If you approach them as a man they would feel insulted and would remind you of who or what they are before storming away. They will belong to only one person at a time, but will change people quicker than changing clothing. They call the dominant participant their "old man." It is extremely hard to understand why they are homosexuals. There appears to be no other motive than the twisted desire deep within them. They also are a root cause for the disruption of the institution. People will fight over them.

Whether dominant or passive, each is considered homosexual by the other inmates. Dominants don't call themselves such and will fight anyone who does. Nevertheless, both engage in the act.

I cannot give you the thoughts of the homosexual. I can give you my observation of them and their condition. They are unsure, quick to exchange lies, unwanted by most, shunned and rejected by many, fearful of today and tomorrow, unsure of even yesterday.

Every homosexual I have encountered is a very confused person. On the surface they have appeared confident of themselves, their motives and actions. Yet, when I have spent some time just talking with them, I have found a very confused, unstable child underneath all the pretenses and defenses. Almost as if they were looking for their mother and father and didn't know where to look, or who to look for—like a lost child in a large department store. Fear sets in, and loneliness attacks and motion is suspended as they are gripped by these two. They begin to withdraw from reality. Should they want to come back they must learn the direction. Once back they would still be lost in a sense, and would need someone who is qualified to help them to become "unlost" so to speak. Someone who would help them relive the experience, the original experience, in order to find their mother and father.

I hope this information will help. I've prayed about it. I hope you're better at rearranging and separating than I am at writing. You also get to figure out all the right spellings.

> Your friend,
> A Christian inmate
> (Name withheld by author)

There are basically three kinds of penal institutions in both the federal and state systems throughout the country. With each kind of institution, the incidence of homosexuality varies. The minimum-security camp or detention center is comprised of noncriminal types. These are people who have indeed committed crimes against society but who do not possess the so-called criminal mind and probably will not return to prison once their short term is satisfied. The incidence of homosexuality in such places is insignificant compared to the overall population figures. There is no more homosexuality on the inside than on the outside.

Medium-security prisons where actual lockup takes place will provide for a higher incidence. Roughly 10 percent of the inmates are directly involved in homosexual activity. They run the gamut from real homosexuals (those who are homosexuals on the outside) to "jailhouse punks," and "commissary punks." The real difference between medium and minimum-security facilities is the length of sentence the inmate is serving. However, this is not always followed, as is seen in the case of the young minister.

Maximum-security prisons generally are for the dangerous or violent criminal element. Often, because of crowded conditions, a "lifer" or other long-sentence inmate will be transferred to a medium-security unit due to good behavior. It is in the maximum prisons that the homosexual scenario takes its most insidious form. All that is described in the above narrative is true. The statement of the chaplain is axiomatic. For a young, attractive inmate entering a maximum-security prison, there is certainty of homosexual assault within twenty-four hours of incarceration. Prisons have been this way for thousands of years. There is little hope for change.

The Church Community

One thing is sure, we homosexuals must all learn to rid ourselves of the sense of shame that we have been conditioned to accept from the heterosexual world. Such shame is no longer acceptable to any of us. How could we go on being ashamed of something that God created? Yes, God created homosexuals and homosexuality. [6]—Rev. Troy Perry, Pastor of Metropolitan Community Church, Los Angeles, California

Our concern at this point is with the effect that the Gay Liberation movement has had and is having upon the church at large. In a later chapter we will discuss the nature and response to that effect. Our research indicates that probably no church of over 200 members is without its homosexual constituency. No matter whether rigid fundamentalist or the most liberal of churches are considered . . . and everything in between the two extremes . . . all churches and Christian colleges are included.

Until recently, those who had homosexual feelings or those who were active homosexuals felt deep shame, and under no circumstances would they allow their homosexuality to be revealed. They were (and many still are) in the unenviable position of needing the church, and yet not daring to reveal to it her/his deepest need.

The reason for this attitude, obviously, is the fear of condemnation from the leadership and ostracism from the constituency. One of the reasons that Rev. Perry has come to the conclusion expressed above is because of his discovery that,

> . . . most organized religions have been no more helpful to us than an empty well, to which we have all returned again and again in some kind of forlorn spirit of hope. We who committed ourselves to a homosexual existence grew gradually to accept a feeling that God did not care about us.[7]

This is an indictment that the church, sooner or later, must face and confess to be true. The shame of homosexuality is far exceeded, in this writer's view, by the shame of failure to love. It is only through realizing this that the church can really begin to hold out hope.

I do not agree with Mr. Perry's position relative to God's creation of and acceptance of homosexuality. But my feelings certainly identify with his sense of rejection. It is really too bad that we Christians who are supposed to be characterized—indeed, known by—our love and Christlike acceptance of people with all their sins—are so prone to reject not only the problems people have, but the people themselves.

Troy Perry has since founded a church for homosexuals which has mushroomed into a denomination. In a conversation I had with Rev. Perry, we discussed pertinent information regarding homosexual involvement within the Body of Christ. Here is the interview in its entirety, except for irrelevant amenities and one area regarding his former wife and his children which he requested to be off the record:

MORRIS: . . . Troy, I have some questions that I would like to ask you. Most of them have to do with your work and what you are doing. I have two that are personal . . .

PERRY: Paul, would you be willing to come to my office . . . ? Are you calling from Los Angeles?

MORRIS: I am calling from Catalina Island.

PERRY: I would like to meet you in person. I'll tell you why. You are affording me a courtesy that some writers from some of the evangelical publishing houses don't give me, and that's to phone me or talk to me personally. But there is a gentleman who has just written a book for the _____ Press for the _____ denomination, that our attorneys tell us is slanderous and we are getting ready to sue them—and that's a first for us. We have never done that. Normally we just ignore things like that, but this one is so slanderous, he is so far out in left field . . . he starts off by talking about the founding of Metropolitan Community Church and just stating a lie . . . saying that when I started the church I called it The Church of the Sodomites . . . and then later changed the name to the Metropolitan Community Church to legitimize the movement. Of course, that's just not true and our attorneys for the fellowship tell us that is slanderous and it is libelous and that we do have a lawsuit.

MORRIS: Well, Troy, I'll be glad to come over and talk to you. I want to assure you as a man and as a Christian, that my interest, while not agreeing with your position . . . is totally in the spirit of love. I do not want to hold you up to scorn, I do not want to examine you under the microscope of prejudice . . .

PERRY: If you hold me up to scorn and it's an honest scorn . . . that I'm not bothered with. It's like I said, this author I couldn't believe . . . the statements he makes are just ridiculous. Even theologically we might disagree . . . that's fine. I don't mind that at all. But it's just the situation, Paul, where I want to make sure the facts are correct . . . If coming to my office is not possible, I'm willing to talk to you, but I want to make sure that what we say is what we say . . .

MORRIS: Two things I would like to say to you: First,

I run the same risk that this other author did . . . I don't want to be sued . . . (laughter)

PERRY: Of course not . . . and from the tone of your voice already, I know you are a Christian and I don't think that would be a profitable . . . thing . . . (laughter) . . . I have a feeling you would not be in the category of this other person.

MORRIS: I want to be absolutely honest . . . with what I present . . . and I think I should tell you, too, that this book does not focus upon you as a person or upon the Metropolitan Community Churches. But, you as a person are highly involved and influential and I don't think the book will be complete without some input from you.

PERRY: No problem. But, like I said, this person has never met me . . . and as far as I know, has never been to Los Angeles, has never even talked to one of our ministers . . . and has been just rabid in his allegations . . .

MORRIS: Well, one thing that should encourage you is that most thinking people should see through that sort of thing . . .

PERRY: Of course, we know that . . . but I want to serve notice on people: Be honest in your reporting. I am not bothered by theological differences . . . I understand that a lot of people are diametrically opposed to what I stand for, and that I can handle.

MORRIS: As I read your book there were things in it to which I could not relate, but one thing I could understand and empathize with is the feeling of fear and rejection you and all homosexuals have received from most organized churches.

PERRY: Certainly. If the church had really done their missionary work . . . I don't think that MCC would have ever existed. But they didn't do it.

MORRIS: Troy, I would like to ask the questions now. If you do not wish to answer them, simply say so and that will satisfy me.

PERRY: OK, fine . . .

MORRIS: How large is your local church?

PERRY: The local church in Los Angeles has a membership of a little over 800.

MORRIS: This is a cross section of the society . . . it is not necessarily all homosexuals . . . ?

PERRY: That's correct. About 15 percent of the local congregation is not homosexual. Let me throw some things out to you: The membership of our denomination, and I am the general executive officer, the title is Moderator. We have 107 churches now.

MORRIS: What is the exact name of the denomination?

PERRY: The exact name is THE UNIVERSAL FELLOWSHIP OF METROPOLITAN COMMUNITY CHURCHES (UFMCC). We are listed in the yearbook of American and Canadian Churches, put out by the National Council of Churches. As of last year's General Conference, our total membership was 20,741.

MORRIS: Do you preach a message that calls for a decision to receive Christ?

PERRY: Let me say this, we are an evangelical church. We believe in a born again experience . . . we preach that. We preach that you have to make a decision for Christ. We do that in a lot of ways. I come from a Pentecostal background. That flavors some of our congregations. Some of our ministers ask people to come forward as a commitment of their faith in Jesus Christ. We are a sacramental church, too. We practice communion every Sunday. We ask people to come forward and receive communion. We say, "Come forward for communion this morning. We know that many of you have stopped years and years ago. You haven't been, but if you have accepted Jesus Christ as Lord and Savior, and you have heard the message preached, we invite you to come forward." There is an altar call, where people come to an altar and we pray with them, and a profession of faith is made. They come forward as a witness to that as the Baptist Church does. Or, they receive Christ through the sacraments themselves . . . they come forward and let the minister know that they have accepted Jesus Christ and then they make an appointment to come in and talk about baptism.

MORRIS: What denominations have been most sympathetic to you and to your church and to homosexuals in general?

PERRY: (laughter) That's a hard question. I'll tell you why. I don't know of any denomination that has taken a stand supporting Metropolitan Community Church. There are denominations that have concerned themselves with the advent of MCC—they have been forced to examine this whole problem for world revival of gay people who want to be attached to Jesus Christ, wanting to make a profession of faith, and finding that, yes, they *can* be a Christian and a homosexual too. One denomination that has recognized this is the United Church of Christ, which, of course, made its stand this last week . . .

MORRIS: They made a stand this last week?

PERRY: Yes. At their General Conference. They went on record supporting legislation for gay rights, but also setting up their commissions which say that homosexuals are persons of worth and moving one step closer to saying that homosexuals, if they are qualified, should be ordained to the ministry of the church.

MORRIS: Troy, what is your response to those Christian homosexuals who have been "delivered" by Christ from their homosexuality?

PERRY: Well, my word to them is this, I say God bless you. I don't believe that you can be "delivered" from your homosexuality, but I believe that you can suppress your homosexuality. I believe that Jesus Christ came and died for my sins—not my sexuality. I do not cease being a sexual person just because I become a Christian. I don't believe that's required by Scripture. What I do believe is required by Scripture, is loving relationships between two people. If it is a loving and not a lustful relationship, then I can't find anyplace in Scripture where that is condemned.

MORRIS: Do you believe that the Scripture, wherever possible, should be interpreted literally, grammatically, and historically?

PERRY: In the original language. I think we have to go back to that.

MORRIS: Do you have a background in the Greek language?

PERRY: Very little. But there are theologians in the denomination with extensive training.

MORRIS: Are you a graduate of Moody Bible Institute?

PERRY: No. I attended Moody, but did not graduate there. I attended other Bible schools as well. I attended Bible college for exactly a year and a half and I make no bones about that.

MORRIS: Deep in your own spirit, now that you have come this far, do you ever really wonder whether or not you may be wrong? Do you ever wrestle with guilt feelings?

PERRY: (brief pause) No. (laughter) I can honestly say that. I can honestly tell you, Paul, that before the Lord . . . I feel like this . . . I feel like God certainly called me to the ministry . . . and at that time . . . you know, here I was with all of these feelings . . . I knew I was different . . . I really couldn't put a label to my feelings but I knew I was different. I felt like, "O God, you've got to change me, because the church has said that . . . these funny feelings I have . . . they are just not right . . . and I used to pray until I was blue in the face. And in my Pentecostal church I believe I received such training and it was fantastic training . . . and then when I was excommunicated from the church, my heart was broken. I felt like . . . I became very bitter . . . I felt like I would never become involved in the church again . . . and I remember that I sort of told God, "God, don't bother me and I won't bother you . . . let's just call it quits because I know what I am now and that's just not going to change." But the Lord let me know later that, "Troy, I love you." I remember saying to God, "I don't know what this beautiful feeling is I have inside, but it just can't be right, because the church says it isn't right." And the Lord spoke to me in that still small voice and said, "Troy, don't tell me what I can and cannot do. I love you. And you're my son." And the Lord instructed me to read the Word and reread again . . . and I believe with all of my heart that I am in the perfect will of God. In the past, I was in God's permissive will and it was a training period. And I really feel good, and, no, not once have I ever questioned, nor have I ever looked back. I've seen people redeemed. I've seen alcoholics delivered. I've seen the sick healed. I know what God can do. I've seen the conversion experiences . . . people who thought they would never know the Lord . . . and that means everything to me.

So there you have it. This ecclesiastical phoenix rising from the ashes of Sodom . . . Probably no Christian church, cult, or ism has enjoyed the phenomenal growth that the Metropolitan Community Church has since the day of Pentecost. It cannot, will not be ignored. Its leader may be nothing short of the Moses of the gay community leading his people to the promised land of social and religious acceptance.

The heterosexual Christian is now forced to declare himself and reaffirm or discard his beliefs about what the Scriptures teach. Homosexuals are no longer hidden safely in their closets out of sight. No longer are they out of mind. You, dear reader, must decide how you will respond to this new profile. Whatever you and I decide to do, and however we respond, let us remember this: We—you and me—we are *not* part of the Trinity; we are not God; the final evaluation—and the only judgment—rests with him.

Legal Implications

There was a time when homosexuals picketed in front of the White House, peering disconsolately through the gate. Now they have stood within the walls of the Oval office, conveying their grievances to the President of the United States. Members of a strong homosexual lobby are visiting our legislators constantly. In some states and cities they wield enormous political power when voting as a bloc. What started the Gay Liberation movement? How did it become one of the most organized social action forces in the country?

What started Martin Luther King?
    What started any of the liberation movements?
    All we want is the same thing the blacks want—equal rights. Why is my life so different from yours other than what I do in my bedroom?
    Why should I be fired from my job because of my sexual differences?
    Why should I be refused housing?

In an interview with one homosexual activist, these disturbing questions were fired at me in rapid succession. I responded,

"Are you saying that oppression started the gay movement?"
    "You bet it did!"

At this writing, forty-two states still have sodomy laws. Should they be repealed? If challenged before the Supreme Court, would they be struck down? In all probability, except where there are large supportive power blocs, legislation supporting the homosexual cause will not be forthcoming. This leaves the courts. Given the activism of the American Civil Liberties Union, already on record as supporting the human rights of homosexuals, the Supreme Court might soon be handing down a decision based upon our revered Constitution.

In a decision with a number of other couples meeting together for this purpose, Dennis Guernsey, Ph.D., close friend, fellow author, educator, and psychologist, presented a disturbing thought; here is how the conversation went:

DENNIS: To what extent should we as Christians try to control the private lives of other people? We make some very fundamental assumptions in this society based on humanism, having to do with the freedom of the individual and his dignity and worth. Constitutionally, we cannot impose the will of the majority upon the minority. We make assumptions about race . . . for example, a landlord cannot discriminate with regard to who lives in his building on the basis of race, religion, or creed . . .

MORRIS: But Dennis, the choice in this case is not one between racial and philosophical differences, but between amoral and moral differences . . .

JAN: But the homosexuals say that it is *not* a "moral" choice.

DENNIS: That may be . . . anyway, that kind of discrimination is now illegal, so are we saying that he should be able to distinguish who lives in his building based on his sexual preference?

MORRIS: Once again, you're putting homosexuality in a category with race, religion, and creed. That, to me, is where the breakdown occurs. There is nothing wrong with being black. There *is* something wrong with being homosexual.

RON: This is essentially the problem. This is how the homosexual cause gets mixed up with the human rights issue . . . it's just been a natural thing . . . what we believe about race, religion, and creed, we simply carry over into the area of morality without a breath.

DENNIS: I'm telling you that this is where the reasoning is going. I think this [the repeal of the Dade County ordinance preventing discrimination because of sexual preference] has shown them that they can't do it legislatively. They will take it to the courts now . . . *what really may be the problem is that the Constitution may be wrong.* The Constitution may not be biblical. Maybe we Christians must admit that to ourselves—maybe the Constitution is guaranteeing things that really are not biblical . . . we can't say that something is right because it is Constitutional. It may well be that homosexuality is a guaranteed constitutional right!

Which, when it comes to legal implications, is about the bottom line.

What I have been trying to do in this chapter is to draw a circle around the problem. Homosexuality and its acceptance poses a vociferous problem to a society predominantly made up of heterosexuals. *Or is the heterosexual phalanx quite so large as we thought it was?* Many researchers of this subject have concluded that both heterosexuality and homosexuality are learned processes; that our sexual preference is determined by our conditioning and that either is as natural as the other. Others claim that homosexuality is like being left-handed. Most of us are aware of the cultural taboos popular not too many years ago, about being left-handed.

I have a theory. I believe we are *all* potential homosexuals. Some call this being polymorphous. I do not mean this in the sense that we all have homosexual desires which we have, for whatever reason, suppressed. On the contrary, it is my contention that heterosexuality is chromosomal and genetic, while homosexuality is symptomatic of pathogenic psychotrauma—a contention which I will demonstrate in later chapters. But I do believe that all persons, male and female, are vulnerable to this psychotrauma. No one is exempt. And as our human predicament becomes more congested, as our anxiety level increases with the crime rate and the inflation rate, more—not less—evidence of this and many other psychotraumatic symptoms will be expressed.

But all is *not* lost!

There *are* effective remedial solutions.

There *is* light at the end of the tunnel.

CHAPTER TWO
CLINICAL DEFINITIONS AND ETIOLOGY

What, precisely, is homosexuality? According to many authorities, there is no such thing—which is another way of saying that it cannot be defined. It is true that there are many shapes and sizes of homosexuality and homosexuals. Latent homosexuality, for example, assumed a technical meaning of suppressed homosexuality, i.e., someone with homosexual tendencies who, for whatever reason, has never expressed them. *Lesbian* is the common name for female homosexuals, while no special name exists for male homosexuals.

Disregarding the prejudicial and derisive designations like queer, fruit, faggot, and three-dollar bill, the homosexual community answers to a number of labels including butch, queen, and drag queen for males, and dyke for females. Each of these designations carries a specified meaning, but the broadest and most inclusive word used by the homosexual community to refer to themselves is *gay*. The etymology of this usage of the word *gay* has no doubt been lost forever. The fourth definition listed in the American College Dictionary for this word is "dissipated; licentious."

No matter. Whatever the assorted meanings, implications, and innuendoes of this jargon, all refer to people who *prefer sexual relations with members of the same sex*. This is the common denominator, and for our purposes, *homosexuality* will be defined as a *symptom* of neurosis expressed by an erotic impulse toward members of the same sex. A *homosexual,* obviously, is a person whose erotic impulse (sexuality) is characterized by homosexuality.

By this definition then, bisexuals or ambisexuals are,

in fact, homosexuals. And latent homosexuals are, in fact, homosexual. It is crucial at this point *not* to depersonalize an individual because he/she is homosexual. Such people are first of all *individuals* and *persons,* with emotions, intellect, will, and priceless human value. It is important to note also that homosexuality is not to be identified with trans-sexualism. This will be explained in detail in a later chapter.

I have always found it repugnant and demeaning to classify individuals according to their behavior. But for the sake of ease in discussion and to aid in our understanding of homosexual behavior, may I suggest the following as a means of identification:

Proclivitic Homosexuality

The person who is a *proclivitic homosexual* believes and functions in what to him is a natural expression of his sexuality. He is completely disaffected or repulsed by the thought of sexual relations with members of the opposite sex. His erotic impulse is totally same-sex oriented. He cannot remember being otherwise. As far as he is concerned, he was born homosexual. For him, homosexuality is just as natural and normal as heterosexuality is for others.

Optional Homosexuality

The *optional homosexual* is a person who has made a deliberate choice to opt for the gay life-style. He is a person who has functioned successfully with emotional and physical satisfaction as a heterosexual. For reasons of experimentation or for a host of other reasons, he has chosen to engage in homosexual sex. Such a person usually does not begin with a homosexual erotic impulse, and this is the major difference between him and the proclivitic homosexual. He "discovers" by experimentation that sex with members of the same sex is, in fact, pleasant.

Not being "true" or proclivitic homosexuals, these people either become so deeply ingrained with the homosexual experience that they become proclivitic, or they become so mentally tortured that they "opt out," or revert back to heterosexual experience.

Having set up definitions, we now ask, how does one become a homosexual? Is it true that some are, in fact, born homosexual? In deep distress of spirit one homosexual said to me, "Why did God make me this way?" Our conversation lasted for some time, and over and over this question came up. Why? Why? Why?

It may come as a shock to many of us, but there are hundreds of thousands of homosexuals who are proclivitic and have maintained a heterosexual existence. This man, a widely recognized Hollywood personality who asked not to be named, had raised two families. But sexually, he was miserable. You have to admire a man who has the mental discipline to successfully suppress his sexuality that long. But for most, it is not discipline, but fear of rejection which motivates the suppression.

The Genetic Argument

But it is one thing to say that a homosexual is proclivitic, it is quite another thing to say that his proclivity is *genetic!*

If it is true that some people are constitutively homosexual and that homosexual relations allow for mutuality, then, from the viewpoint of Christian theology, it is the task of homosexuals to acknowledge themselves as such before God, accept their sexual inclination as their calling, and explore the meaning of this inclination for the Christian life.—Gregory Baum, Catholic theologian

All too true! But that is a very big "if," indeed. There are very few scientists today who believe that homosexuality is in some way genetic or hereditary. There is a cogent reason for this. There is no evidence for it whatsoever. The theory that homosexuals are born, not made, has become vaporous. Male homosexuals have, science now proves, the normal X and Y chromosome count— those Barr bodies that define men as men, not women; their gonads are fertile and their hormones healthy. After thirty years of testing blood samples from homosexuals, researchers have discovered nothing. One's race, size, color of hair and eyes, and gender are all genetically determined. All of this has been scientifically substantiated. But in all of the experimentation and investigation, scientists have no evidence that a homosexual is so because of genetic and biological constitution!

Dr. Arthur Janov, a brilliant psychologist, who has enjoyed unparalleled success in the treatment of homosexuals remarks:

I do not believe that there is a basic genetic homosexual tendency in man. If this were true, the cured patient would still have his homosexual needs, which he does not. Post-Primal patients who have been latent and overt homosexuals before report no homosexual leanings, fantasies, or dreams. Judging by the way male and female parts fit together, it seems to make sense that given a healthy body, there is only heterosexuality.[8]

There are, however, many homosexuals who believe that they are the products of genetic configuration. Among the most ardent in their commitment are the homosexual Christians. The reason for this, obviously, is their desire to credit God with their homosexuality. If God is really responsible, then all of the passages in the Bible which discuss the subject must be reevaluated:

Now I know that I'm opening Pandora's Box when I tell you that I'm sure that homosexuality is pre-ordained. I think a lot more work has to be done in this whole field, but I am firmly convinced that much of what we are comes to us through our genes. I know that many people will throw up their hands in horror and say: "Why, where could you get such an idea? Where's your proof? Where's the data to support your stand? Where are your experiments? And what theological reasoning or anything else could support such an idea?" Well, I'll just draw a blank. I just believe it, that's all.—Troy Perry

Convenient. Like being saved. One just believes and he is. Only with salvation, believers are provided with some credible standard—namely, the Scriptures. I am sorry, Mr. Perry. Your subliminal neurosis is a pretty shaky foundation upon which to construct a theological argument, not to speak of Truth.

But what about hormonal disturbances? These do occur. Individuals are often born with male/female hormonal imbalances. Can these be causes of homosexuality? The theory of hormonal imbalance has alternately gained and lost support over the years. Recently, sex researchers Masters and Johnson have investigated this theory (1971). The problem with it is that while an imbalance is found in some homosexuals, it is not found in most. Moreover, there is the possibility that the hormone imbalance is the *result* rather than the cause of the psychosocial disorientation. Under conditions which produce anxiety and uncertainty, the same imbalance may be provoked in persons who are otherwise heterosexual.[9]

The Conditioned Response Argument

One recent religious writer has made a case for what he calls the *condition* of homosexuality as distinct from the homosexual act itself. The idea is that because of certain lifetime and environmental experiences, a person may be conditioned, in the Pavlovian sense, to respond homosexually. While the theory regarding conditioning is certainly true, I prefer to avoid the term *condition* in favor of *proclivitic*. This is because it is the neurosis that is the condition—not the homosexuality. Condition implies a set, irreversible posture, while a proclivitic symptom certainly does not.

Whatever the semantic gymnastics, it is a fact that neurosis, for the most part, is the result of early childhood, infant, and in some cases, *prenatal* trauma. Couple this with sexual identity confusion imposed upon a child by external influences (parents, friends, etc.), and you have a *prima facie* genesis for homosexuality. This is what happened, in my opinion, in Troy Perry's case (as is evident from the biographical material in his book).

But it is important to note that the result of the condition is *neurosis*—not homosexuality. One may be involuntarily and unconsciously "led" into homosexuality by very subtle influences, but it is in concert with neurosis and a series of catalyst traumas/experiences that the symptom occurs, and without the neurosis it would not occur. More about this under the heading of *The Neurosis Argument.*

The Demon Possession Argument

A paragraph on this subject is justified because there are readers who may have serious questions about it. In my research, there is no evidence that homosexuality is the result of demon possession. Biblically, there is compelling evidence that for the Christian, demon possession is impossible. Also, demon possession is characterized by attendant phenomena which are absent in the case of most homosexuals. This is not to say that homosexuals cannot be possessed of demons, but rather that homosexuality *per se,* is not the result of demon possession.

Jim Kaspar, who is the director of EXIT (Ex-gay Intervention Team), a ministry of the Melodyland Christian

Center's Hotline program located in Anaheim, California, remarks, "We haven't met anyone who has gone into homosexuality because of the demon of homosexuality. We have met those who have experienced oppression from spirits who also happened to get into gayness." Mr. Kaspar informs me that 8 percent of all hotline requests are from homosexuals seeking help, which coincidentally, corresponds with the percentage of those who are exclusively homosexual in the overall population.

The Neurosis Argument

Your childhood is really much worse than you ever thought it was . . .—Michael Holden, M.D.

The concept that homosexuality is a symptom of a deeper neurosis is, in my view, the only valid pathological generalization. Neither scientists, nor anyone else, have isolated a homosexual virus. Homosexuality seems to have a hundred contributory dimensions. But it is, as evidenced in my clinical studies and what seems like countless personal conversations—a symptom of a *deeper aberration:* be it neurosis, the condition of sin, or primal pain.

It is crucial to make the point that there exists no certain formula for specific neurosis. One set of stress stimuli may be completely shrugged off by one person while virtually destroying another. Much depends upon the specific emotional constitution of the individual in question. It can be said that some of the best adjusted, non-neurotic people have come from a holocaust childhood. And others who have had serene, non-stress childhoods have become neurotic. But we are talking here about almost microscopic percentages. The plain fact is that almost all of us can be placed somewhere along a graduated scale of neuroticism.

I am convinced that neurosis begins very early in life.

Perhaps even in the womb. In some cases this can be remarkably demonstrated. In my earlier volume, *Love Therapy*, I tried to document the immense contribution to the study and healing of human trauma made by Dr. William Glasser in his concept of *Reality Therapy*. And in these pages I would be remiss if I did not mention the work being done by Dr. Arthur Janov and his associate, Dr. Michael Holden, M.D., in the healing of neurotic pain. Dr. Holden is a neurologist and is the Research Director for The Primal Institute in Los Angeles.

In a lengthy conversation with Dr. Holden, I was apprised of a case in which a patient actually had "Primal scenes" which involved his actual birth.

. . . I sincerely believe that homosexuality is always neurosis and it is always due to very early pain . . . catastrophic pain very early in life . . . perhaps even before birth for some children . . . certainly within the first month of life. This patient had many scenes relating to the delivery room. He was rejected by his mother practically from the moment of his birth and was warmly embraced by his father within the first day of his life . . . he has had that scene many times in his Primals . . . that embrace from his father. Now he understands his own homosexuality as an attempt to get back to the good feeling of that embrace on day one of his post natal life. So for him the sequence was a catastrophic and total rejection by mother followed by a very good second best from his father and spending the rest of his life trying to get some warmth from men.

Prior to the birth experience, neurosis in the fetus can be induced by maternal trauma. A fall, great emotional stress, premature birth, and a host of other stimuli can plant the seeds of neurosis in the psyche of the yet unborn child. This became evident in a question and answer session with Janov and Holden in which the question was put:

QUESTION: Dr. Janov, how does a child become neurotic in the womb? Can the mother's emotions be transferred physiologically to the child?

JANOV: I'm going to shift this to Dr. Holden. I think he's qualified to answer it.

HOLDEN: I think the point to emphasize is that if a mother is stressed, that stress reaction on the part of the mother has a physiological basis: more secretion of steroid hormones, more secretion of adrenalin, tense musculature in the abdomen. And the baby, of course, is going to be aware of that.

QUESTION: Do the steroids go into the baby?

HOLDEN: Most of the molecules in the adult's bloodstream do cross the placenta. There are some which do not. But a small molecule like adrenalin certainly does. And for instance, one of the well-studied effects of maternal behavior on the physiological state of the fetus is in relation to smoking. Smoking decreases the oxygen level in the mother's bloodstream and physiologically deprives the child of an adequate oxygen supply. This is thought to underly the observation that children born to mothers who smoke heavily are one or two pounds lighter than children born to mothers who don't smoke. It's a trauma to the child.[10]

All of this is to demonstrate that neurosis can be induced into the human fetal state . . . however, let us be aware at this point that all we have is an unborn neurotic baby—not a homosexual baby. But the stage *is* being set.

After the child is born, his neurosis is broadened by continued stress—stress that parents generally do not comprehend. In fact, the result of that stress—crying—becomes a stress course for the parents; and the vicious, damaging circle begins. Parents however, suffer far less from this cycle than the child. Babies can choke, gasp, cough, cry, vomit, scream, stop breathing, have seizures, and have an inner body crisis when they are hurt (spanked or pummeled). They can't run away. They can't light up a cigarette, or take a drink, or a pill, or find a sexual release, or even pray. In addition to relying on a considerable defense structure they have erected over the years, parents can do all the things the baby can do, as well as pursue all of these sublimative escapes.

Dr. Holden told me that:

The pain a baby endures in the first six months of his life, even with so-called standard up-bringing . . . I mean just not being picked up in the crib for a two-month-old child . . . is a catastrophic pain. *One may cry about that for fifty or sixty hours in therapy* [italics mine] . . . a single event of being abandoned in the crib. So that the valence of these early pains, the amplitude or the charge value, is incredibly high . . . and it's those early pains which I think really set the pattern for one's life. In that Freud was absolutely right . . . we become neurotic—*definitively*—within the first few days and months of our life. And the pattern is set for all later compounding of pain.

In another place Dr. Holden makes a forceful point:

We need to put to rest once and for all the myth that babies do not feel pain or remember it. The truth is, babies feel more than we adults do. Much more. That central fact, based on a timetable of brain maturation, plays a major role in the genesis of neurosis. Until we treat babies like very sensitive human beings, generations will continue to be born internally wracked by early life Pain and suffering which most often surfaces as chronic psychosomatic illness. There is no other way to prevent neurosis in people except to meet their real needs when they are little people.[11]

As he grows, such a child is immensely susceptible to homosexual stimuli. The pain that he feels pushes him—indeed drives him—toward relief . . . relief which only can be found in a loving milieu. Homosexuality may derive from any number of family intrarelationship permutations. A homosexual boy can have a weak father, tyrannical father, no father. The relevant factor is that the boy lacks a *loving* father. There is little need to examine these relationships in psychotherapy. What must be reached is the *need*. It is the need that is being acted out in homosexuality.

The homosexual act is not a sexual one. It is based on the *denial* of real sexuality and the acting out symbolically through sex of a need for love. A truly sexual person is heterosexual. The homosexual has usually eroticized his need so that he appears to be highly sexed. Bereft of his sexual fix, his lover, he is like an addict without his connection; without his lover, he is in the Pain that is always there but which is drained off sexually. But sex is not his goal—love is.

The homosexual is usually the tensest of all neurotics because of how far he has been made to go from his real self. The tension can drive him to liquor, drugs, and compulsive sex, and these outlets are still not enough. Many homosexuals I have seen report psychosomatic complaints. The violence we see in homosexuals is the result of self-denial. When a person cannot be what he is, he is angry.[12]

In the case of proclivitic homosexuals, early and prenatal childhood pain is a common denominator. This, coupled with confusion in sexual identity by inadequate parental role modeling and inadequate love sources, produces someone who does not remember when he was ever heterosexual—thus his conclusion that he is biologically constituted as a homosexual; and in the case of a religious person—that God created him that way.

In the case of the optional homosexual, his symptom has taken longer to surface. When he makes his conscious decision to try the homosexual life-style, he is seeking to be loved . . . the same motivation germane to the proclivitic homosexual. But in his case, he is not "truly" homosexual. He is a heterosexual who is disoriented in his heterosexuality due to his basic neurosis, and stimulated by his environmental factors. This is, in fact, the case with the proclivitic—but in his case, his disorientation occurred too early in life to make his homosexuality anything but what is, to him, a *natural* experience.

The Pathogenic Psychotrauma

If you have ever wondered why doctors and scientists use these silly multisyllabic words, it is because: each syllable has a meaning. And, when they are strung out together, they form a convenient description of the subject in question. Such is the case with *pathogenic psychotrauma*. Besides having a good, sound, informed ring to it, it means: *patho*—suffering feeling; *genic*—genesis, production, development, origin. Put together, the word means the origin and development of suffering or disease. *Psycho*—having to do with the psyche or the mind (religion: *soul*); *trauma*—injury. Together it means injury to the mind. The whole phrase means the traumatic origin(s) of psychological suffering.

It is precisely this background which, in my estimation, forms the soil and the explanation for homosexuality. I have already pointed out that homosexuality is a symptom of neurosis. But why homosexuality in particular? There are many symptoms of neurosis. How does one's neurosis find expression in homosexuality?

The answer: *Homosexual trauma* affects the sexuality structure in the mental/emotional framework. Consider: the individual is already traumatized and neurotic. When events unfold which contribute to his sexuality dysfunction and identity confusion, the individual's neurosis is influenced—molded by these events like soft clay. A homosexual pressure is exerted on this soft clay, leaving a distinct impression, and another, and another . . . and the clay hardens. These pressures are traumatic, not necessarily in the emotionally violent sense; but injury is caused just the same, in the same way that accumulative and gradual radiation negatively affects animal tissue.

It is my opinion that a kiln is involved—a catharsis. There is a time when the accumulated pressure of these traumas increases the temperature of the tension to a white heat—and then a catharsis occurs which hardens the neurotic into the homosexual form, in which case he begins to think and act like a homosexual. He sincerely believes himself to be sexually oriented to persons of the same sex. In some cases, especially in today's moral climate, he may opt for an open homosexual life-style; in other cases he may prefer to keep his homosexuality closeted or suppressed; and if his moral or spiritual sensitivities have not been too severely seared, he may reach out for help. He will be seeking to be loved. (In which case we believers had better be ready to respond.)

God has already given them his love.

CHAPTER THREE

THE "GAY" WORLD

A note for the squeamish: this chapter may be ugly and offensive. I lived through it and I can attest to its sordidness better than anyone. It was difficult enough to couch these homosexual life experiences in words acceptable to my readership. But, read this you must—and I apologize in advance for any rape of spiritual sensitivity that may occur.

I have never spent much time on the streets of San Francisco. It is where my wife and I honeymooned. We stayed in a beautiful motel and saw all the sights and ate at the nicest restaurants. San Francisco has more internationally known restaurants than any place in the world, with the possible exception of Paris. During the summer of 1976, my wife and I returned to San Francisco—this time with our children. Once again, we saw the sights, ate at the restaurants, and rode the cable cars. Occasionally, we saw two men walking down the sidewalk holding hands. We glanced away, deliberately opting out of drawing conclusions. Nobody said anything. Nobody commented.

I read the newspaper. Our Sony violates our living room with the unpleasant details about the city whose voting population is approximately 28 percent homosexual. It seems impossible to me. For you see, while I am a distant observer of the streets of San Francisco, I was a *part* of the everyday scenario on the streets of Long Beach. About half the size of San Francisco, Long Beach is the largest city of the Los Angeles basin metropolitan complex. I have a hard time understanding how San Francisco—or any city—can have more homosexuals *per capita* than Long Beach. It was there that "Bob 198" became the extension of my body, my mind, my personality. "Bob 198" is a 1971 Checker type taxicab.

Learning to drive a taxicab is an interesting experience.

I did it as a matter of economic necessity—not by choice. Two years before, I had completed my advanced graduate degree and was at that time the minister of a small, struggling mission. The church had started in my home and had grown out of that, and I felt a certain sense of commitment to it. But the financial reward was minimal. I had to supplement my income. So, I labored for the church during the daylight hours, and at night, until 3 A.M., for almost a year, I drove "Bob 198."

At first they teach you the basics: how to use the radio, operate the meter, help the passengers, make out the trip ticket, handle the money, find all the taxi stands, etc. What they did not tell you about was the life of a taxi driver. They did not tell you that the job is more dangerous than being a cop. They did not tell you that most of your clientele were the poor, the oppressed, the criminal. They did not tell you that in order to survive, you had to become callous, insensitive, and tough. All of this for $125–$150 a week, including tips.

Someday, I think I will write a book about my taxi experiences. But I would have to do so under a pseudonym. It would ruin me professionally if I revealed all of the sordid things that happened, and how I responded to them. Many of the readers of *this* narrative will find enough to give them chest pains and nausea. If not, then perhaps you are better suited for that job than I was.

But I didn't do badly. I learned the ropes quickly enough. I learned how to protect myself (I carried a bowie knife with an eleven-inch blade, a police baton, and a .380 caliber baretta). I learned how to hang tough, and the word didn't get out that I held a fancy Ph.D., until a couple of months before I was scheduled to quit. By that time all the guys had accepted my "street credentials," and it didn't seem to bother them. I got my share.

Violence

"Bob 198!" The graveled voice of the dispatcher shorted out my dreams and stopped my head from nodding. It was 2 A.M. Morning breath fouling my mouth, I angrily snatched the microphone from its mount on the dash and spoke into it,

"Bob One-Ninety-Eight." I was glad the dispatcher couldn't smell.

"L'l Lucy's. Get the bar keep."

"L'l Lucy's," I mumbled back and hung up the mike. Complaining to myself as the engine chugged into life, I pushed the old Checker down Broadway toward the gay bar. It was only one of a few dozen gay bars I knew about in the city. It would not surprise me to learn that I am the only Christian, not to speak of Christian minister, who has been in all 500-plus bars in the city of Long Beach.

The red-orange neon sign was still on as I approached the bar. Half a block away, it went out. The bar was closed. I pulled the cab up in front and sat on the horn. I waited. It was an old one-story red brick building. The windows were boarded up, and except for the sign and the dilapidated front door, one would think it was abandoned and condemned. In a few minutes a thin figure appeared at the door, clad in an old Army "Ike" jacket and denims, with a red bandana tied around his head. His beard was thick, red, and bushy. He was the bartender and he was gay. How did I know he was gay? Because on occasion he went drag. I was startled one night when a woman got into my cab and spoke to me in a husky, male voice. It was him.

He approached the cab, peered through the front door passenger window and tried the handle. It wouldn't budge.

"Get in the back!" I yelled. "It's against the rules to ride in the front when the back seat is empty." He got into the back seat, glared at me for a moment, and said, "1944 Magnolia." It was the address of his semi-suburban house.

I said nothing, making the notation on the trip ticket, which took about thirty seconds. I was just putting the trip ticket away when he said:

"You going to sit here all night? Let's get going!"

Again, I said nothing, threw the flag on the meter, and nosed the cab out into the traffic lane. At the next street I made a left turn and he spoke again,

"You're the SOB who blows his horn in front of my house, aren't you?" This was with contempt and hostility.

I slammed on the brakes and he lurched into the back of the front seat. I turned to him, and for the first time, spoke:

"Get out! I don't have to take this kind of abuse and I'm not about to."

"Aw, man, don't make me do this . . . I've got to get home . . . I'm tired, man . . . I'll keep my mouth shut . . . please . . ."

It was a halfway decent fare and probably the last one of the night for me, so I decided to chance it. I said nothing, turned around, and drove off. I adjusted the rearview mirror so I could look him directly in the face, just in case. He was true to his word; he said nothing else for the rest of the trip. Only every time I glanced at him in the mirror, he was glaring at me.

I pulled up in front of his house and stopped. I kept the motor running. He got out and came around to my window. Still glaring at me, he fumbled with his wallet and paid me. When I gave him his change, I said in what I hoped was a conciliatory way:

"Thank you very much, sir. Have a pleasant evening."

He turned to leave and I turned to complete the trip ticket. What happened next only took a few seconds.

He yelled . . . no, it was more like a scream, and lurched at the taxicab. Out of habit, I had already opened the door enough so that it could swing free without hanging up on the lock. This is a trick one learns early in cab driving experience. That door can be a formidable weapon as well as an effective shield. When he got to the cab door, the window being down, he whipped out what seemed to me to be a switchblade of giant proportions, and hissed through his teeth:

"Hey, sucka', I'm gonna make you so you have to sit down to urinate!"

I am not Mike Hammer . . . nor Superman. I was a thirty-eight-year-old man with a suburban home, a lovely wife, and three beautiful children. And I want to tell you something, I was scared numb. I do not have iron fists or scars on my face from my fights with Russian spies. I like to cut the lawn, pray, go to church, and live peaceably. I am a mild, warm, personable creature who likes to help people.

In this situation, I had no time to reason or pray . . . only react. Unknown to this guy, I had a pretty good rebel yell myself, and out it came; the door slammed into his face, into his knife, which flew from his hand, and into his body, which flattened him on the lawn in front of his house. And out I tumbled from the cab with the hilt of the eleven-inch bowie in my hand. The next scene I remember was me standing on that guy's neck with my left foot (I had seen some cops do this downtown), and I laid the sharp edge of the blade along the bottom of his nose. Now it was his turn to be afraid.

He did not move.

"Stay still," I commanded, and wondered where the words came from. He could only grunt in response. I was hyperventilating. Finally, I could feel some of the effect of the adrenalin wearing off, and I relaxed. I took my foot off his neck and said,

"Stay where you are. I am going over and getting in that cab and driving off, and if you so much as twitch a whisker, I'm going to come back here and we'll see which one of us gets to sit down to urinate." Slowly, I backed away; he lay still. When I reached the cab, I got in and drove off. When I looked back, he was still lying in the yard.

By the time I arrived at the barn, I was much calmer. But it took a bit of aimless driving to achieve that. The supervisor came out and said:

"Say, Paul, what happened at that Magnolia address?"

"You mean with that homosexual [euphemism] dude?"

"Yeah. He just called in. Said you pulled a knife on him . . . said you almost killed him. I asked him why you would do something like that."

"What'd he say?"

"He hung up."

"Good night, Virgil."

"Good night, Paul."

Filmmakers, both pornographic and otherwise, are capitalizing on the trend toward violence in our society. The ultimate in pornographic movies nowadays is something called the "snuff film." It is alleged that in this kind of movie, a victim is actually killed during the filming; this always is in connection with a sexual situation. According to many psychologists, the move toward violence in our country is a sexual aberration.

The homosexual community is not without its contribution. The incident described above is not an isolated one. One of the primary male motivations in the male homosexual milieu is pure machoism: men who are trying to prove (to themselves) their masculinity. This may seem paradoxical at first glance, but much of homosexuality is, after all, a male ego-trip—men seeking sexual dominance over men. Many times this is accompanied by violence or by the threat of the symbols of violence. The fierce-looking beards, the knives strapped on the hips in plain view, the steel-studded black leather jackets, and the chains . . . all contribute to the image that a certain segment of the homosexual community is violence prone.

These are the butches. While driving the cab, I often had to enter a gay bar to make contact with a fare. In all of them there were the butches—the sergeants-at-arms slouching in the corners, giving the "I'm baaad," look to anyone who would glance their way.

How large is this segment? Nobody really knows. Based on my one experience and contacts, and the experiences of the homosexuals I interviewed, it ranges anywhere from an estimated 10 percent to as high as 30 percent of the total gay community. However, the butches are really only representative of the hostility that most homosexuals feel. It's this substratum of hostility which prompts the violence. It is the same sort of hostility found in the ghettos which prompts mugging, rape, looting, and murder. The violence we see in homosexuals is, in all probability, the result of self-denial. When a person cannot be what he is, what he subliminally wants to be, he is angry.

Homosexual violence is a fact. In the social activists' attempts to present a more palatable image, this fact will be disclaimed or made to appear irrelevant. To be sure, there exists the upper echelon type of homosexual, and the businesses which cater to such types. And this harmless, professional, affluent image is the one that society will accept as being typical of the gay life-style. But it is not typical. It is the exception.

In some of my interviews with homosexuals in preparation for this book, the violence problem was downplayed.

Asked if violence was ever a part of their homosexual experience, some said yes. Most said no—that they avoided it wherever possible—that homosexuals were lovers, not fighters. Some had been raped by much larger "butch" types, some had had rape attempted, others were involved in sadomasochistic violence.

If the rest of society follows the example of San Francisco's school board, it is hoped by this writer that the total picture will be considered. If the violence profile—in my opinion, very much deserved—of the homosexual community is swept under the rug, it will be a very serious error in judgment.

There will be those who will argue that homosexual violence is no more or less than that evident in the rest of the population. I disagree. I offer in rebuttal my experience on the streets, my clinical studies and research, and the testimonies of those homosexuals who seemed to enjoy the telling of it. And another reason: unlike the family for the heterosexual community, the basic social unit for the homosexual is the *gay bar.* There you will find no risk imposed by the responsibility of children . . . only pounding, blaring music, promiscuous sexual involvement, booze, violence, and . . . vomit.

There is no doubt that stable, responsible homosexual relationships do exist. But this is the exception—the *rare* exception—not the rule. Studies have demonstrated that these relationships tend to be transitory. It is no wonder, given the environmental basis for their social involvement.

It is interesting to note that the Scriptures themselves have not let this aspect of the homosexual life go unnoticed:

. . . the men of the city, even the men of *Sodom,* compassed the house round, both old and young, all the people from every quarter; and they called unto Lot, and they said unto him, "Where are the men which came in to thee this night? bring them out unto us, that we may know [have sexual relations with] them. And Lot went out at the door unto them, and shut the door after him, and said, I pray you, brethren, do not so wickedly. Behold now, I have two daughters that have not known [had sexual relations with] man; let me, I pray you, bring them out unto you, and do ye to them as is good in your eyes: only unto these men do nothing, for therefore came they under the shadow of my roof. And they said, Stand back. And they said again, This one fellow came in to sojourn, and he will needs be a judge: now will we deal worse with thee, than with them. And they pressed sore upon the man, even Lot, and came near to break the door . . .—Genesis 19:4–9

The Homosexual Bar

I do not want to labor this aspect of the gay world. But I do want to reinforce the reality that the gay bar, is, indeed, the fundamental unit of the gay society. This is where more than 95 percent (an educated and *very* conservative estimate), of the homosexual population interact initially with each other. I have not talked to a single homosexual or former homosexual (unless he/she was of the most rigid closet variety) who was not a common visitor of the gay bar.

What goes on at a gay bar? In deference to those gay persons who are not part of this scenario, I want to say that I have not been in every gay bar in the world, or even in every gay bar in the Los Angeles metropolitan complex—but I have been in every known gay bar in the city of Long Beach.

In what way are these bars different from heterosexual bars? That will be seen in what follows, but make no mistake about it, there is a substantial difference. There may be some who will say that this really isn't very scientific. I do not believe this to be true. What better laboratory can a scientist have than one which provides the reality as it happens, uncontrolled . . . noncontrived? Here are my observations:

Drunkenness

Frankly, not very much drunkenness goes on in the gay bar. Not nearly so much as in the heterosexual bar. This is because of the endemic hostility of homosexuals. When they get drunk, they get mean. But when it does happen, it is nauseating and ugly. I have been struck by a pool cue, vomited on, spit at, abused verbally, and vilified for being "straight." Quite naturally, you will understand that I sometimes left the bar without receiving my fare. Most of the people I picked up from heterosexual bars were drunk or well on the way. Only occasionally did I have to haul away a drunk from a gay bar. But when I did, it was a bummer.

Promiscuity

Another reason why drunkenness has a low profile in a gay bar is because heavy alcohol consumption tends to retard sexual activity. And for what the gay bars do not have in drunkenness, they make up for in sexual activity. Again, this is not seen nearly as much in the heterosexual bar. In gay parlance, the word for it is "grab." This means genital fondling through clothing. I have seen this being done on adjoining bar stools, at tables, inside telephone booths located in the bar, and on the dance floor. I have witnessed "French kissing," embracing, and almost constant hand-holding. Please do not conclude from these remarks that everyone in a gay bar is doing this all the time. But enough of it does occur to be highly visible to an outsider.

Cliques

Another phenomenon which distinguishes the gay bar is the cliques. The queens and the drag queens associate together. The butches, the dopers, the socially elite, etc., all may attend the same bar, but they segregate. This is perhaps more noticeable to the homosexual who visits the bar than to an outsider, because it is necessary for the visitor to find his "group," and he usually finds it quickly because of another phenomenon:

Gaudy Wearing Apparel

The favorite color of homosexuals is lavender or light purple. In fact, the Gay Liberation movement is often referred to by some newsmen as the "lavender" as opposed to the "orange," (Anita Bryant and her association with the orange juice industry). Psychologically, this color is also the favorite of children and the emotionally immature, according to the Luscher Color Test. At any rate, the clothing worn by homosexuals is often gaudy and bizarre. This is not true, of course, of all homosexuals. The professional and well educated, particularly in their professional environs, are indistinguishable from anyone else. But in the homosexual bar, there is a kaleidoscope of colors.

Same Sex Patrons

This is the most obvious sign that one is in a gay bar. Occasionally one will see a female in a male gay bar. But one never knows whether the alleged female is a drag queen, lesbian (usually this is the case if there are two women sitting together in an otherwise all-male establishment), or an unwitting and naive heterosexual chick. I have never seen a male in a female gay bar. Some gay bars cater to both sexes. These are usually the nicer establishments, but the patrons still segregate. Females dance with females; males dance with males.

The gay bar is the place for social interaction. It is the place to go to "cruise," (look for and solicit a sexual partner), or just find idle chitchat and friendly association. The gay bar is the unique creation of the gay community. Bars are the vessels through which the gay lifestyle flows and gains nourishment. The gay bar is the "family living room" of the gay establishment.

The Bathhouse

"Bob 198." I reached for the mike. I was sitting in my cab watching the lively activity of the Belmont Shore area of Long Beach. Belmont Shore is a beach community where everyone lives within walking distance of a broad, white sandy beach. It was about 10:00 P.M. and I had been on the job about five hours. Belmont Shore is the fun part of Long Beach. It is here the vast majority of young, single career people live. At one time, it was the retirement center of the city. There are still many retirees here, but this section has largely been rented out to the young swinging set. I once lived here myself. Belmont Shore also contains the highest percentage of homosexuals in the city.

"Bob One-Ninety-Eight," I responded.

"Ripple's," came the order.

I knew the place . . . one of the liveliest and most colorful gay bars in the city. I repeated the order back to the dispatcher and kicked the engine to life. As I arrived at the bar, situated on Ocean Boulevard facing the vast expanse of beach, a number of people were milling about on the wide sidewalk in front. As I drove up, two expensively dressed men in their middle forties stepped up to the cab and got in the back.

"Trouble?" I asked, noting the crowd outside.

"Fight," one of them said. This was rare for this place. This bar is one of the nicest, as far as facility is concerned, in the city. Usually, only the affluent came here.

"Uh, take us to the Bath House, will ya buddy?" This would be a good trip, money-wise, for me. With any kind of decent tip, I would clear about ten bucks. The Bath House was across town in the small city of Wilmington . . . on Anaheim Boulevard. As we nosed our way through traffic the two men simply sat in the back and conversed quietly. If one did not know better, one would never suspect that they were homosexuals. But I knew better. I knew because of where I picked them up, but mostly because of where I was taking them.

A homosexual bathhouse is one of the more lurid aspects of the gay world. There are many such establishments scattered throughout the country. They are not nearly so numerous as the gay bar, but every major city, no doubt, has at least one.

John W. Campbell, age forty-four, is described as a wealthy businessman with a pot belly, a cherubic face, and a ready laugh (*Newsweek*, 6/6/77). He also owns a chain of bathhouses. "A shrewd businessman, Campbell bought a Cleveland sauna-bathhouse for $15,000 in 1965 and turned it into a homosexual health club. Within a year, he made enough money to open a second club. Clubs in Toledo, Newark, Baltimore, Atlanta, and other cities came next, and today Campbell's profitable Club Bath chain totals forty gay bathhouses—most with steam rooms, snack bars, music and television rooms, and swimming pools. They also have private cubicles where men can have what Campbell discreetly calls 'relationships.' "—*Newsweek*

Perhaps another description of these places is in order . . . this from a homosexual prostitute:

. . . it seemed to me like a kind of self-inflicted imprisonment. It's full of guys and they think that they can just have you as they want you. Generally, if you're in that mood . . . that's great. You know, I suppose it's wonderful. I've only been in that mood . . . or thought I could do that only once or twice. Mostly . . . I went there . . . there's a lot of Amyl Nitrate * grass, other types of pills

* Amyl Nitrate is a drug used to relax the anal sphincter.

and drugs you could get into if you knew who to ask. It's dark. It's hot and steamy. Guys run around in towels . . . usually if you walk by a room they will make some comment . . . if they like what they . . . thought they . . . see they really can't see you, they can only see what they think they see . . . they see what they would call a huge male stud, they would ask him if they could go down on him . . . give him oral sex . . . maybe not finish the job . . . but you know, a lot of it . . . get him very stimulated and move him on and just try to . . . that's what they all did, it seems like . . . They don't allow booze. Booze makes you open up too much . . . you know . . . you want to be too physical . . . people get hurt when there is booze around and they get loud and break things. There is something like Amyl Nitrate . . . you sniff it, inhale it, and it brings about a giddiness . . . your head feels woozy and you experience a loss of hearing. There is just a bare cot, bare walls with graffitti written on them. They give you a towel. There might be sheets on the beds. There might not.

When I pulled up in front of the Bath House, the men paid me, turned, and disappeared into the gray, dingy multistory building. They did not leave a tip.

Homosexual Prostitution

In the course of my research, I have interviewed two homosexual prostitutes, at different times and under different circumstances. The second instance involved a young man who had opted out of this life-style and now considered himself a former homosexual. (This interview appears in an excerpt in the previous section.)

I have learned a number of items important enough to be mentioned here. First, homosexual prostitution is big business, and it is widespread. The prostitute's primary pickup environment is, of course, the gay bar; and his profession, while lucrative, is not always enjoyable:

. . . sometimes it was absolutely . . . absolutely just as much as I could handle. Sometimes it was just the most

unpleasant . . . I actually just had to sit down . . . and
. . . you know . . . ah . . . say a silent prayer to try to
keep myself from killing the person. I just hated him
so much . . . some people can make you hate them so
bad . . . I just had to be very cold and calm myself
down . . .

For this they get paid an average of fifty dollars a trick.
The orientation and objective of the homosexual prostitute is exclusively orgasm—not for himself—but sometimes for as many as ten men at a time. In my opinion,
prostitutes are the most completely exploited people that
exist. True, they get paid for it, but what happens to
them psychologically and spiritually is virtually irrep-
arable.

Even more obscene is the abuse of children in this regard. An Episcopal priest was recently convicted of turning his farm for wayward boys "into a house of horrors"
by forcing teen-agers to commit homosexual acts for pornographic pictures. "They [the sponsors] took the pictures. They positioned these naked boys in all sorts of
poses and they sent those pictures all over land and sea,"
attorney Joe Bean told a Circuit Court of ten men and
two women. The prosecution opened the case by introducing more than 400 photographs of what it said were former residents of the Alto, Tennessee, facility engaged
in sodomy and fellatio.

And in New York a congressional subcommittee went
into the heart of Manhattan's smut and sex district and
heard horror stories about children being forced—sometimes by their parents—to perform for pornographic films
and books. The House Subcommittee on Select Education
was shown books and magazines depicting children, one
only six years old, in sexual poses. Father Bruce Ritter,
a Franciscan priest who is director of Covenant House,
testified that some of the youngsters shown in the magazines and books had been seduced or forced into filming

sexual activities. Others, he said, had been raped and pressed into white slavery. Father Ritter said his agency has helped 1,000 runaway and stray children in the past year. He told of a "go-go boy" of seventeen who danced in a bar where customers would place bills in his jock strap.

Former Mayor Abraham D. Beame, when he led police on raids against smut shops in Times Square, said, "We have not yet sunk to the level of savage animals, but if we don't draw the line against pornography, we can kiss good-bye to civilization as we know and cherish it."

One other observation germane to the discussion of homosexual prostitution, is the patent narcissism of those who sell themselves in this way. Both of the homosexual prostitutes I interviewed went to great lengths to tell me how good they were in bed and how beautiful their bodies were:

I was very well liked. I'm a very sexy person as far as men go . . . being a good looking guy, I got all kinds of people. Everybody liked to talk to me. I was a popular person. . . . sex with men . . . I was really good at it . . . I'm very good at prostituting my body because I'm very sexy . . . I'm nice to look at. . . . I'm nice to talk to. I'm five eleven. I'm nicely muscled. But I'm muscled in a rather delicate way. I have a good chest but I have thin wrists and large hands. My legs are very nice. They are as nice as a woman's legs. I'm very graceful. I'm as graceful as most women. I'm very good looking. I have very piercing green eyes. I have short-cropped, nice-looking hair. And when I move, I excite people . . .

All this and more in the course of one conversation.

The Lesbian

Lesbianism is treated here because of its own unique contribution in the gay world experience. Lesbian bars *per se* are very few in number (only two in Long Beach). And they are exclusively female. I'm sure that this is not the case in all female gay bars, but the ones with which I am familiar seem overpopulated with the "dyke" or masculine type of lesbian. I do not wish to abet a stereotype here, but the lesbians who patronized the exclusively female gay bars in my city were of the most unattractive type—masculine types with a heavy build, short-cropped hair, no lipstick or other cosmetic attentions, and hair where you do not often see it on women.

But this by no means completes the picture of the lesbian world. Kinsey estimates (and this is an obsolete estimate—prior to the "sexual revolution" and the feminist movement), that 12 to 13 percent of all women have sexual relations to the point of orgasm with other women sometime in the course of their adult lives. Kinsey further estimates that 11 to 20 percent of single women and 8 to 10 percent of married women have made at least some homosexual contact or association.

In our research, we have discovered that lesbian relationships tend to be less transient than those of gay males, and tend to involve greater interpersonal commitment. This is because women seem to be more relationship oriented than sex oriented. Further, statistics seem to bear out the fact that, on the whole, women seem to be more sexually successful in lesbian contacts than in heterosexual contacts.

The reason for this is that the woman approaches orgasm with a more equal perspective—unconcerned with "pleasing her man." She feels less obligated to perform to her husband's standard, or what she conceives to be her husband's standard, and more free to experiment and enjoy. We should note, however, that this phenomenon speaks less to the positive side of lesbianism than it illustrates the strong need for heterosexual interplay to be examined and upgraded.

What is "different" about sexual relations between women is precisely that there is no one institutionalized way of having them, so they can be as inventive and individual as the people involved. Perhaps the two most striking specific differences from most heterosexual relations . . . were that there were generally more feelings of tenderness, affection and sensitivity, and more orgasms. This higher frequency of orgasms in lesbian sexuality has of course been remarked on by other researchers going at least as far back as Kinsey. Also lesbian sexual relations tend to be longer and to involve more over-all body sensuality, since one orgasm does not automatically signal the end of sexual feeling, as in most heterosexual relations . . .[13]

While what this researcher observes may indeed be true, it would be missing the point to conclude from this that women should become more involved in lesbian activity. The emphasis should be upon improving heterosexual relations. One of the reasons heterosexual dysfunction occurs with many women is because of a power struggle. Seeking sex with women can be a reaction against men and the alleged second-class status of women in this society. For some women, sex with a woman means independence from men.

Shere Hite, in her report on female sexuality, has come to a horrendous moral stance with regard to lesbianism. Hers is the only otherwise responsible research I have encountered which openly *advocates* the lesbian experience. It makes one wonder about Shere Hite:

It is important for women to recognize their own potential for having sexual feelings for other women. If we want to grow strong, we must learn to love, respect, honor, and be attentive to and interested in other women. This includes seeing each other as physically attractive with the possibility of sexual intimacy. As long as we can relate sexually only to men because they are "men" (and as long as men can relate only to women because they are "women"), we are dividing the world into the very two classes we are trying to transcend.

Any woman who feels actual horror or revulsion at the thought of kissing or embracing or having physical relations with another woman should reexamine her feelings and attitudes not only about other women, but also about herself. A positive attitude toward our bodies and toward touching ourselves and toward any physical contact that might naturally develop with another woman is essential to self-love and accepting our own bodies as good and beautiful. As Jill Johnston has written: ". . . until women see in each other the possibility of a primal commitment which includes sexual love they will be denying themselves the love and value they readily accord to men, thus affirming their own second class status." [14]

Whatever this philosophic and pragmatic gem may say about the motivation and/or objectives of the feminist movement, I leave for my reader's imagination.

All of this leads us to one final observation regarding lesbianism: it is less proclivitic than male homosexuality, and more optional. This may appear at first glance to be contradictory to the fact that lesbian relationships are less transitory. But the point is that our research is strengthened by the evidence that there are disproportionately more optional lesbians than proclivitic lesbians. Either type may form strong liaisons. But for the reasons just cited, there are more women who opt for the homosexual life-style than feel they were homosexual from birth, or have positive sexual aversion to heterosexual activity.

The Transvestite

Transvestism may or may not be homosexual in character. It simply means someone who dresses up in the clothing of the opposite sex as a sexual expression. A "drag queen," or one "going drag," is a male homosexual who is dressed up to appear as much like a female as possible. But there are men who will do the same simply for the sexual titillation of doing so. These men are heterosexuals; they have no desire for same-sex activity. Their reason for dressing like women is not to attract other men or to have sex with men. Such people are often called "transvestites."

Transvestism occurs primarily in what amounts to the most sexually frustrating period of male development: adolescence. Such activity has nothing to do with masculinity—only erotic arousal. In preparation for masturbation, boys will sometimes dress up in panties and brassiere and view themselves in a mirror. Most boys will do this at least once in adolescence, never to repeat it in adulthood. A survey of 500 adult transvestites (Prince and Bentler, 1972) found that about half commenced crossdressing prior to puberty and about half during early teen-age years. This data does not indicate how many other males cross-dressed earlier in life but abandoned the activity.

Transvestism in adults is a symptom of neurosis relating to sexual dysfunction or frustration. It is important to realize in this study, of course, that it is *not* same-sex oriented. The objective is self-arousal; unless, of course, the subject is suffering a pathological psychotic episode.

Closet Homosexuals

If a homosexual has not declared himself openly and publicly as such, he is often referred to as a "closet homosexual." Nobody knows, except his lover(s), that he is homosexual. In our society, this description fits virtually all homosexuals at one time or another in their homosexual life. But as has been indicated, in recent months, the doors have been swinging open.

The Homosexual Church

A discussion of the gay world would be incomplete if it did not include a section on one of the strangest phenom-

ena in this whole strange way of life. I refer to the homosexual church. Frankly, as churches go, it is not very
large—having only a little over twenty thousand members throughout the country. But its influence has been
significant. In fact, it has probably provided the Gay Liberation movement with its "moral" impetus. With the
advent of the homosexual church, came also the mitiga-
tion of the shame of being a homosexual—through acceptance of the belief that God was not only no longer mad
at them, but that he approves of and is the creator of
homosexuality. This line of reasoning also showed up in
the militant black power and women's liberation groups,
who decided that Jesus was black and God was a female!
Homosexuals have not yet collectively advanced the theory that Jesus was gay, but (as we shall see in a moment)
they point out that there is ample reason to believe he
was.

The only recognized force in this aspect of the gay world
is the Universal Fellowship of Metropolitan Community
Churches. Its founder and chief executive officer (Moderator), is the Rev. Troy Perry. Perry, for all practical purposes, has not been educated either biblically, theologically, or ethically in any formal sense. By his own
admission, he received no more than one and a half years
of such education. Presumably, this means three se-
mesters.

A product of the Pentecostal holiness movement, and
one Aunt Bea (whose idea of faith is to hold a large rattle-
snake over one's head while speaking in tongues), Perry
believes that his church background and brush arbor
preaching have adequately prepared him for the ministry. Indeed, there are many "ministers" in charge of congregations who have as much or even less training than
has Perry.

It should be made clear that I am not a critic of those
churches or those believers to whom God has given the

gift of speaking in tongues. I don't really get turned on by rattlesnakes, but in all fairness, neither does Perry. In fact, I must say that from my conversation with Rev. Perry and my evaluation of his book, I readily assent to his warm and engaging personality, his obvious intelligence, and his ability to articulate. It would be easy to befriend such a man.

At this point let me quote a passage from *The Lord Is My Shepherd, and He Knows I'm Gay*. It will give us a perspective on the theology of Rev. Perry and presumably, that of UFMCC:

. . . I saw this lady coming determinedly up the street. I held out a leaflet and said, "Here, madam, would you take one of our leaflets?" She didn't say a word. She just hauled off and hit me as hard as she could with her purse. I didn't believe it. So, like a fool, I repeated myself. I said, "Madam, are you sure you don't want one of our leaflets?" So, she hit me again.
She said, "If I had my way all of you perverted individuals would be locked up in jail, and the key thrown away!"
I said, "Madam, that's a wonderful Christian attitude you have."
She looked me over, backed off a step, and I thought she was going to hit me again. She said, "Young man, do you know what the Book of Leviticus says?"
I told her, "I sure do! It says that it's a sin for a woman to wear a red dress, for a man to wear a cotton shirt and woolen pants at the same time, for anyone to eat shrimp, oysters, or lobster—or your steak too rare."
She said, "That's not what I mean."
I said, "I know that's not what you mean, honey, but you forgot all of these other dreadful sins, too, that are in the same book of the Bible."
She said, "Do you know what Saint Paul said?"
I said, "I sure do. He said for women to be silent, not to speak."
She said, "That's not what I mean either."
I said, "I know it's not, honey, but Paul disliked women: he said that women were not to teach, preach, and that they were not to have any sort of authority over a man. Where would our women's liberation groups be if they had listened to the apostle Paul? He didn't like women with short hair, nor men with long hair. He said, 'If a

man have long hair, it is a shame unto him, but if a woman have long hair, it is her glory.' Are we going to close the doors of the church just because the apostle Paul didn't like women with short hair, nor men with long hair?"

She said, "That's still not what I meant." I pressed on:

I said, "I know it's not, honey, but you know Paul was a very generous fellow. He met a slave one time, and the word of God says that he converted this slave, made him a happy *Christian* slave, whatever *that* is. Well, he didn't try to get him to Canada via the Underground Railroad. He sent him back to his master *still a slave!* Paul wasn't against slavery. You know he was cited as the principal reason for the Southern Baptists to split away from their church in 1845, and found their organization, just so they could keep their slaves.

Yet today, no one in his right mind would quote the apostle Paul to justify his right to maintain slaves or slavery."

Then she took out of that heavy purse a small, but hefty, Bible. She said, "Read this, and see what Paul said to the Romans."

Well, some think I never passed my examinations at that Bible College I went to, but I did. I shut her Bible and handed it back to her and I recited from memory exactly what he said in Chapter One, Verses 26–28. I said, "Here they are, madam," Paul's epistle to the Romans, Chapter One, Verses 26–28:

For this cause God gave them up unto vile affections. For even their women did change the natural use into that which is against nature: And likewise also the men, leaving the natural use of the woman, burned in their lust one toward another; men with men working that which is unseemly, and receiving in themselves that recompense of their error which was met. And even as they did not like to retain God in their knowledge, God gave them over to a reprobate mind, to do those things which are not convenient . . .

"And, in First Corinthians, Chapter Six, Verse Nine:

Know ye not that the unrighteous shall not inherit the kingdom of God? Be not deceived: neither fornicators, nor idolators, nor adulterers, nor effeminate, nor abusers of themselves with mankind . . .

"And, further, in First Timothy, Chapter One, Verses Nine and Ten:

Knowing this, that the law is not made for a righteous

man, but for the lawless and disobedient, for the ungodly and for sinners, for unholy and profane, for murderers of fathers, and murderers of mothers, for manslayers, for whoremongers, for them that defile themselves with mankind, for men-stealers, for liars, for perjured persons, and if there be any other thing that is contrary to sound doctrine . . .

"And I'll agree, madam, Paul did not like homosexuals, but Paul did not take to women's rights, and he would be appalled at short hair on a woman, or excessively long hair on a man. Now, if we're going to close the doors of the churches to the hippies just because they have long hair, and to women who have short hair, or wear a red dress, or eat those forbidden foods, or who teach, or preach, or who exercise any sort of authority over a man, where would we be?"

She said, "All right, smarty, what did Jesus say?"

I said, "Now according to the way you think and act, He would have been a real weirdy—for you. If He lived in this day and age the way you people label individuals, you would have labeled *Him* a homosexual right off the bat! I don't believe that Jesus was a homosexual. But I know you people. Here was a guy raised by a mother with no father—typical of the homosexual syndrome, according to so many psychiatrists (for what that's worth)— He never married, and ran around with twelve guys all the time. Not only that, He wasn't above having bodily contact with another man: John the Beloved lay on the breast of Jesus at the Last Supper. Not only that, but a *guy* betrayed Him with a kiss! Doesn't that make you want to throw up? Not once did Jesus say, 'Come unto me, all ye heterosexuals . . . and you can become true followers.' No! Jesus said, 'Come unto me all ye that labor, and are heavy laden, and I will give you rest.' And that includes homosexuals, too. God doesn't condemn me for a sex drive that He has created in me. He doesn't condemn me unless I leave the areas of love and go into the areas of destructive excessive lust."

Well, she was as white as a sheet. She just stood there, staring at me. I went right on, "When Jesus was asked what is the great commitment, Jesus didn't talk about homosexuality or heterosexuality. He said this, 'And thou shalt love the Lord thy God with all thy heart and with all thy soul, and with all thy mind, and with all thy strength: And the Second is like unto the First, 'thou shalt love thy neighbor as thyself.' And I think that's the gospel according to Jesus Christ. If I follow the Word, and those gospels, and I am brought to God and saved from my sins, not saved from my natural sexuality, then I believe I am a Christian and I am saved.

"While we're at it, in Romans, Chapter Fourteen, Verse Fourteen, it says, 'I know and am persuaded by the Lord Jesus that there is nothing unclean of itself: but to him that esteemeth anything to be unclean, to him it is unclean.' And in Titus, Chapter One, Verse Fifteen, it says, 'Unto the pure all things are pure: but unto them that are defiled and unbelieving is nothing pure!' " [15]

Again, in fairness, we should recognize that the above conversation is not a well-thought-through, documented, theological treatise. It is, however, submitted here as typical of the religious thought offered to justify the homosexual theological position. It is interesting to note in this regard, how Perry has thrown the "Are you really saved?" football back into the laps of those who question the eternal destiny of homosexuals. The last biblical statement to which he refers seems to imply in this context that to those who are genuinely pure, all forms of behavior (things) are pure. The obvious implication is that if this is not, indeed, the case, then one is defiled and unbelieving. So if one is to disapprove of homosexual behavior, he might well have reason to hold his own salvation suspect!

But what of the homosexual who is also a professing Christian? In the light of Paul's remark in 1 Corinthians 6:9, 10, can a practicing homosexual "inherit the Kingdom of God?" If we are going to accept this biblical statement at face value, then in addition to homosexuality, we must include all of the other things named both in this passage and in Galatians 5:19–21, where Paul names the "works of the flesh." And if we say that nobody fitting these descriptions will inherit the Kingdom of God, then our Lord is going to be rather lonely. None of us is going to make it!

There isn't a mother's son among us who hasn't sinned

or who does not sin—daily! If that isn't practicing sin—what is? Of course, there remains the question of one who deliberately intends to sin—no matter what God thinks. But what if one redefines a specific sin to be something good—something God created? Obviously, this *is* a convenient resolution of the problem.

Even so, the facts are, if God is going to base our entrance to heaven upon our sterling behavior—it just isn't going to wash for any of us. And so, for us who are made of flesh and blood, and whose feet are of clay—for us to make judgments about the eternal destiny of another such person—is just plain stupid! If a man professes a belief in Jesus Christ, I want to say that God has not given me, nor has he given anyone else, the credentials to question the genuineness of that profession. Maybe there are "tares among the wheat," but I can't tell one from the other and, for the record—*neither can you.*

One more observation about the homosexual church: has anyone received Christ as a result of the ministry of its constituency? If Mr. Perry is telling the truth, we must say, yes. This does not mean that God created homosexuality. This does not mean that all their ridiculous claims about homosexuality and the homosexual act are true . . . but it does mean that the homosexual church is doing a job for Christ that the organized, established church has not done for almost two thousand years! And if I were Mr. Perry, I would feel pretty good about that.

CHAPTER FOUR

THE VIEW FROM THE BIBLE

Two basic questions face us at this point: first, is what the Scriptures say relevant? Second, assuming it is relevant, how shall we interpret it?

To many, of course, biblical instruction on homosexuality is little more than a curious literary viewpoint, and to some perhaps, it doesn't even merit curiosity. But to those who feel strongly about the subject, the biblical narratives are indeed of interest. And to the church, what the Bible has to say is crucial. It is from the Bible that the church draws her theology and guide for faith and its practice. So if the Scriptures address the subject of homosexuality, the church by definition must accord them credibility.

But how are these passages to be interpreted? There are at least two distinguishable hermeneutics (systems of interpretation) often resorted to by the various and often opposing factions of the Body of Christ. The first hermeneutic we shall call *cultural*—which is to say that the Scriptures have no specific present-day application. What is written applies only to the immediate recipients of the literature in question. Interpretation of the Scriptures, with this as a basis, would be highly influenced by their cultural setting. We might, as a church and as individual Christians, see enduring principles at work in these various settings, and learn to adapt these principles for our own profit. But we dare not apply the assorted imperatives, injunctions, rules, etc., in any sort of direct form, as though they were written with us in mind.

The second hermeneutic we shall call *literal.* This interpretive principle allows us to accept the teachings of the Scriptures across the board, and to make specific applications to present-day believers. Those who adopt this view generally make room for cultural influence, but point out that the Bible was written for all men during every age. They accept the Bible literally except when it is impossible to do so; as in some of the apocalyptic passages or those sections dealing with the punishments/rewards of a specific biblical nation or people.

There are weaknesses in both hermeneutics. The first permits the relegation of all biblical phenomena and instruction to the cultural scene. In other words, it would be possible to say that *none* of the Bible is meaningful in any present-day context. It leaves it up to the interpreter to decide what is and what isn't. Often, this is decided in a very arbitrary fashion. On the other hand, the literal hermeneutic raises the specter of legalism. It places the unsuspecting believer into a box-like, push button, knee-jerk relationship to God. Irreconcilable biblical conflicts arise, which in order to solve, he must go in the direction of the cultural, historical hermeneutic. And so, with most reasonable theologians, both viewpoints give way to the demands of the other. In this way, a measure of unity and strength is worked out, and polarization is diminished.

With respect to the biblical issue of homosexuality, the two viewpoints come into striking conflict. The extremists which accept only the cultural viewpoint (Metropolitan Community Churches; the authors of *Human Sexuality,* a study commissioned by the Catholic Theological Society of America; the United Church of Christ, et al) culturalize the biblical narratives in such fashion that the sinfulness of the homosexual act loses most, if not all, of its sting. The literal extremists make homosexuality the most repugnant, the ugliest, the absolute worst of all possible sins, resulting in such rhetoric as . . .

So-called gay folks [*would*] *just as soon kill you as look at you . . .* —Rev. Jerry Falwell, as quoted in *Newsweek*

Homosexuality is a sin so rotten, so low, so dirty that even cats and dogs don't practice it. . . —Rev. Jack Wyrtzen, as quoted in *Newsweek*

The sad part of all this is that each end of the spectrum can interpret the Scriptures to its own satisfaction—both denying the credibility and legitimacy of the other, each pointing out the other's weaknesses, each rationalizing or ignoring his own weaknesses.

Where does this leave you and me? The first thing we should do is begin by admitting that *isolated* analyses of individual passages do not produce binding, convincing evidence that homosexuality is wrong. Perhaps there may be enough evidence there to convince you and me—but not necessarily someone with a different set of presuppositions or a different prejudicial bent.

Let me give you an example. In the Romans passage (1:26, 27), the operative phrase being, ". . . and likewise also the men, leaving the natural use of the woman, burned in their lust one toward another. . ." This phrase and its immediate context, in the minds of most interpreters, clearly is the strongest passage against homosexuality in the Bible.

Yet homosexuals view this passage entirely differently. They maintain that this passage has reference to those men who consciously gave up their heterosexuality in favor of homosexuality. They feel it is not speaking of a natural or proclivitic homosexual. It could be said, they allege, that the principle taught by this passage could be likewise applied to a homosexual who gave up his natural homosexuality in favor of heterosexuality! Those who do not write Paul off as being hung up sexually, say that in all of his writings Paul does not condemn homosexuality *per se*, only lust—which may be expressed either homosexually or heterosexually.

Ridiculous? Absurd? Maybe so. But *plausible?* Definitely. Viewed from the homosexual perspective, this passage actually *supports* those homosexuals who claim to be naturally so. So, when "God instructed" Troy Perry to reread the Scriptures, this is the kind of interpretations which resulted. *Or,* in the case of Paul and his prohibitions against homosexuality, since the church widely ignores many of Paul's other prohibitions and relegates them to the cultural grab-bag—why not homosexuality? *Or,* if homosexuality is just another sin among so many—some of which all of us commit—why all this fuss over it? I mean, what right have we straight Christians to judge or condemn the homosexual? We are just as much guilty of sin as he. *Or,* homosexuality is sin only if we think that it is. Didn't Paul say that if a man esteems something to be sin that for him it is? So, if you are not already a homosexual, don't practice it . . . but if you are, by all means, be what you are without shame or apology. *Or,* . . . the Old Testament passages? Don't be silly. They were meant for Israel along with all of the other dietary laws and those laws associated with that nation only. *Or,* . . . Jesus? Jesus never said a single word about homosexuality! So there!

Disturbing, isn't it? The arguments we have used so many times in our efforts to dislodge our opponents in order to maintain our own theological distinctives are coming back to haunt us. How many times have we used these same arguments with regard to divorce, baptism, long hair on men, short hair on women, female ministers, prayer bonnets, dancing, movie going, mixed swimming, *ad infinitum* . . . ?

In addition to the passage from the first chapter of Romans, there are at least three other passages suggested by Christian homosexuals to support their position. David and Jonathan's relationship is highly suspicious (1 Sam. 18–20). Even before there was a creature like a gay Christian, the homosexual overtones of this passage had been discussed. Saul's son, Jonathan, is now held by many gay Christians to be definitely homosexual, and the best that could be said about David is that he was bisexual. (In this connection, one person even suggested that Ruth and Naomi could have been homosexual.) Jesus spoke of eunuchs, "which were so born from their mother's womb" (Matt. 19:12). Conceivably, a natural-born eunuch was homosexual. And finally, Paul said that it is *good for a man not to touch a woman* (1 Cor. 7:1), and that "there is . . . neither bond nor free, there is neither male nor female" (Gal. 3:28). What more evidence do we need to justify the credibility of the Christian homosexual?

If people would look at gays as being Christians and sons and daughters of God—accept us for what we are—that God loves us as much as he loves them, then we could have a much, much better united Christian community, . . . instead of looking in the Old Testament and other passages and concluding that homosexuality is a sin. Homosexuality is not a sin. That's the way I feel. I feel I can worship my Lord. I can get down on my knees . . . and when I get to heaven, I just hope that day of rejoicing will be as happy for us then, as it is for us now, knowing that we can be accepted by God.—Dave Richards, deacon MCC, Los Angeles

Specifically, what *does* the Bible say about homosexuality? What are the passages? Perhaps it would be best to allow the passages to speak for themselves. As you read them and think about them, try to gather together a general impression of all the passages taken in concert. After doing that, try to measure the force or the intensity of that impression, if in your mind it is distinct enough, on a scale of say, 1—10. Think also about the context in which they occur, and what influence that should have on your interpretation. Do not consider the literary context only, but also the context of the historical situation.

See where *you* come out. Only the passages which are distinctly homosexual in character are presented here.

Genesis 18—19: The Story of Sodom and Gomorrah

The story of the destruction of these two cities on the plain near the Dead Sea is, of course, well known. God had made the decision to destroy the cities because of the enormity of their sin. Yet, he told Abraham that he would not do so, so long as there were at least ten righteous people left in the city. Abraham's nephew, Lot, and his family lived in the city of Sodom. Now, Lot was anything but a righteous man, if we define *righteous* in terms of the lack of evil in his life. As we shall see in a moment, Lot was a *very evil* man in terms of his deeds. But Lot did love God. And even then, God did not so much determine righteousness on the basis of the lack of evil deeds, as he based it upon love for God and faith. So by this latter definition, Lot was indeed a righteous man—and so the Lord sent two angels disguised as men to rescue Lot and his family from the coming destruction. It is at this point that we encounter the operative passage:

And there came two angels to Sodom at even; and Lot sat in the gate of Sodom: and Lot seeing them rose up to meet them; and he bowed himself with his face toward the ground; and he said, Behold now, my lords, turn in, I pray you, into your servant's house, and tarry all night, and wash your feet, and ye shall rise up early, and go on your ways. And they said, Nay; but we will abide in the street all night. And he pressed upon them greatly; and they turned in unto him, and entered into his house; and he made them a feast, and did bake unleavened bread, and they did eat. But before they lay down, *the men of the city, even the men of Sodom,* compassed the house round, both old and young, all the people from every quarter: and they called unto Lot, and said unto him, *Where are the men* which came in to thee this night? bring them out unto us, that we may know [have sexual intercourse with] them. And Lot went out at the door unto them, and shut the door after him, and said, I pray you, brethren, do not so wickedly. Behold now, I have *two daughters* which have not known man; let me, I pray you, bring them out unto you, and do ye to them as is good in your eyes: only unto these men do nothing; for therefore came they under the shadow of my roof. And they said, Stand back. And they said again, This one fellow came in to sojourn, and he will needs be a judge: now will we deal worse with thee than with them. And they pressed sore upon the man, even Lot, and came near to break the door.—Genesis 19:1–9

Lest there be any doubt, the sin in question here is most certainly homosexual in character. The verb "to know," as used here and elsewhere, means "to have sexual intercourse with." Then we observe, 1. The angels in question were recognized as men. 2. The *men* of the city desired to have sex with these men—by force (rape) if necessary. 3. Lot generously offered them his virgin daughters to satisfy their sexual craving. 4. Note: The men of Sodom *rejected* the females *in preference for the males.*

A recent study of human sexuality commissioned by the Catholic Theological Society of America has been hailed as an authoritative, scholarly work destined to have major impact upon the moral posture of the church. However, the credibility of its scholarship is somewhat shaken by these curious observations:

. . . Even more ominous was the punishment visited by God upon Sodom for the *assumed* sin that was named after that ill-fated city. As often as it refers to the sinfulness of Sodom, the Old Testament never explicitly identifies Sodom with the practice of homosexuality. In fact, there is no uniform tradition as to the nature of Sodom's offense.[16]

It should be noted that this volume does not carry the *Nihil Obstat,* or the *Imprimatur,* which is to say that it does not carry the official approval of the Roman Catholic Church.

One of the favorite points made by homosexual Christians is that Jesus never said anything about homosexuality. Since the Genesis passage clearly indicates homosexual activity and intentions, it is not difficult to understand the implication of our Lord when he remarked:

. . . but the same day that Lot went out from Sodom it rained fire and brimstone from heaven, and destroyed them all . . .—Luke 17:29

. . . which is to say that Jesus understood the wickedness of Sodom; in particular, its homosexual wickedness. On at least two other occasions our Lord referred to Sodom, but in these instances he was comparing the lesser sin of Sodom with the greater sin of the modern cities (Capernaum, et al), which rejected him and his disciples. An interesting thought for those who consider the homosexual act as among the worst of all possible sins.

One other passage worth mentioning regarding the sin of Sodom is found in the seventh verse of the epistle of Jude:

Even as Sodom and Gomorrah, and the cities about them in like manner, giving themselves over to fornication [immorality], *and gone after strange flesh,* are set forth for an example, suffering the vengeance of eternal fire . . .

If Jude had meant simply rape (as some claim the only sin of Sodom to be), or adultery, or for that matter, homosexuality, he could have stopped with the inclusive word, *pornaia,* immorality. But the phrase, "gone after strange flesh," set in a sexual context, and given the already demonstrated nature of Sodom's sin, is unmistakable.

Leviticus 18:22; 20:13: The Mosaic Code
Thou shalt not lie with mankind, as with womankind: it is abomination.

And if a man also lie with mankind, as he lieth with a woman, both of them have committed an abomination: they shall surely be put to death; their blood shall be upon them.

The first thing that should be said here is that the Mosaic Code, with its attendant sanctions, cannot be applied specifically to the Christian church. The homosexuals are absolutely right in their assertion that if we are going to subscribe to the Mosaic Law, then we must also subscribe to its sanctions, i.e., impose the death penalty, in this case, on homosexuals. So, the church does not pledge its allegiance or its obedience to the Law, be it moral, ethical, or dietary.

But this does not mean that the Mosaic Code does not contain rules, ideas, precepts, and guidelines by which we live, and which are major doctrinal distinctives of the Christian church. The church adopted them not because they are recorded in the Mosaic Code, but because they are universal, eternal principles governing the relationships of mankind. If the Mosaic Code did not now exist, nor ever had existed, these principles would be self-evident and in firm and binding effect.

What this passage does reveal is that homosexuality, in the Mosaic economy, is among those things which God rejects—which, indeed, are an abomination to him. The mind of God with respect to homosexuality is not confined to this one statement in the Law of Moses; but this statement *is in harmony* with God's predisposition against homosexuality recorded elsewhere in the Scriptures.

1 Samuel 18 ff.: David and Jonathan

This passage is mentioned only because it is advanced by the religious homosexual community as an instance of an approved homosexual relationship. The passages of particular focus are:

Then Jonathan and David made a covenant, because he loved him as his own soul. And Jonathan stripped himself of the robe that was upon him, and gave it to David, and his garments, even to his sword, and to his bow, and to his girdle (1 Sam. 18:3, 4).

And as soon as the lad was gone, David arose out of

a place toward the south, and fell on his face to the ground, and bowed himself three times: and they kissed one another, and wept one with another, until David exceeded (1 Sam. 20:41).

I am distressed for thee, my brother Jonathan: very pleasant hast thou been unto me: thy love to me was wonderful, passing the love of women (2 Sam. 1:26).

Admittedly, it is easy to read homosexual overtones into these passages. However, anyone who examined the biblical narratives concerned with the lives of David and Jonathan would be forced to conclude that both men were aggressively heterosexual. This rules out any possibility of proclivitic homosexuality, and greatly minimizes the possibility of optional homosexuality.

Further, the homosexual hypothesis is nothing more than speculative. There is no concrete evidence to indicate that the relationship or love these two men shared was sexual or erotic in character. Innuendos obviously can be inferred, but such a basis for theological argument is wispy indeed.

Romans 1:26, 27: The writings of Paul
For this cause God gave them up unto vile affections: for even their women did change the natural use into that which is against nature: and likewise also the men, leaving the natural use of the woman, burned in their lust toward one another; men with men working that which is unseemly, and receiving in themselves that recompense of their error which was meet [due].

1 Corinthians 6:9, 10
Know ye not that the unrighteous shall not inherit the kingdom of God? Be not deceived; neither fornicators [*pornoi*, men involved with prostitution], nor idolaters, nor adulterers, nor effeminate [*malakoi*, men who engaged passively in homosexual acts], nor abusers of themselves with mankind [*arsenokoitai*, men who engage actively in homosexual acts], nor thieves, nor covetous, nor drunkards, nor revilers, nor extortioners shall inherit the kingdom of God.

1 Timothy 1:9, 10
Knowing this, that the law is not made for a righteous man, but for the lawless and disobedient, for the ungodly and for sinners, for unholy and profane, for murderers of fathers and murderers of mothers, for manslayers, for whoremongers [pornois], for them that defile themselves with mankind [arsenokoitais], for menstealers, for liars, for perjured persons, and if there be any other thing that is contrary to sound doctrine.

Even the most ardent biblical literalist will have to admit that interpreting the writings of the apostle Paul is sometimes no picnic. Peter, a member of the inner circle of disciples, and also an author of sacred writings, conceded that Paul was often hard to understand.

Paul's ecclesiastical writings have been the subject of much debate in the church for almost two thousand years. His writings about the church, ethics, relationships, and the like are possibly more responsible than any other body of literature for the schisms, sects, and denominations that we have today. But this does not mean that we must relegate all that Paul said into a hodge-podge of negotiable potpourri. There are things which this writer of Scripture has to say that are clear, unmistakable, and in harmony with specific thematic concepts of the Bible. Homosexuality clearly falls into this latter category. We may push and shove or otherwise negotiate such matters as divorce and remarriage, prayer bonnets, hair length, church officers, women's silence, and the like, but to place homosexuality and the other above-named sins in this environment is to commit intellectual suicide.

What we have been trying to do in this chapter is to present the biblical attitude toward homosexuality and the homosexual act. The Scripture makes no distinction between the two. What it says about the one, it also says about the other. Unless one assumes that one cannot help his homosexual feelings and is therefore not responsible for them, one must conclude that the Bible condemns homosexuality as well as the act.

But to me, the most compelling evidence for a theological stance against homosexuality is simply this: when we weigh the overall biblical evidence, it is heavy. The accumulating trend, the overt statements, and the clear implications are together very forceful indeed. Even the opponents of the biblical picture are in agreement on this fact—even if they rationalize it all away. *But add to this:*

Eden Revisited

There was a time on this planet when there were no homosexuals. We do not know when man first paired off with man, or woman with woman. But we do know, if we accept the Genesis record, that there was a time when there were no homosexuals.

If God created the heavens and the earth, then it is not hard to believe that he could have created a male companion for Adam, capable of reproduction. He did do this in other species. But he did not do it with man. When Adam awoke from his sleep . . . there was a woman. Not another man . . . a woman. A woman. A WOMAN!

There is no question in my mind as to the nature of the first interaction between this first naked man and this first naked woman. It was sexual. *They became one flesh. From that instant on, the natural pattern of things, as God intended them to be, was forever set.* How else could it be? If we had no further statements in Scripture regarding homosexuality or heterosexuality—from this one event alone we would correctly understand the natural order of the true sexual proclivity.

But with the third chapter of Genesis came also a newly deformed sexuality. Thus it became necessary for God to reveal his mind about it in later events and writings.

Look at them together: passages on the sexuality created in Eden and the attendant negativism about homosexuality in later writings. What possible conclusion can a rational man make?

One closing observation. Homosexual theologians and those Christian theologians who support the gay cause, have reinterpreted the passages of Scripture which discuss the subject, with the effect of neutralizing their impact through culturalization, rationalization, or inverted meaning (as in the case of the Romans passage). This is evidence of a curious sense of responsibility and honesty to Scripture, to say the least. One cannot help but recall the passage in the fifth chapter of Isaiah, where it speaks of those who make good look like evil, and evil look like good:

Woe unto them that call evil good, and good evil; that put darkness for light, and light for darkness; that put bitter for sweet, and sweet for bitter! (5:20).

Far be it from me to pronounce woes on anybody! If I began with myself, I would never get past my own navel. And far be it from me to pronounce woes upon my homosexual friends—that's right—friends. But if I were a Christian homosexual, I think this one question would disturb me most: Am I trying to interpret Scripture in the light of my own proclivity; or should I interpret my proclivity in the light of Scripture? It's only fair.

CHAPTER FIVE

TREATMENT

The lyrics of a Neil Diamond ballad tell of a man groping for identity, a man who has emptiness inside. He speaks, but no one listens; and he says he "never cared for the sound of being alone." It is a struggle all of us experience. We are born into this world, sail through childhood, stumble awkwardly through adolescence, and emerge, usually stunted and deformed emotionally, into adulthood still searching for identity.

We develop a sense of dimension. We know our height, weight, and other assorted physical characteristics; we add to our sense of identity through our associations, our relatives and friends; we add still more through our employment and career; and we come to know our gifts, abilities, horizons, and limitations. All of these add to our sense of being. But somehow, through all of this, we often miss our sense of viability and self-worth.

When this sorry state of affairs is fully realized, or sensed . . . we become afraid. We become afraid of ourselves and for ourselves. Anxiety reactions occur. Psychosomatic illnesses invade us like the plague. We have a general sense of being ill-at-ease and insecure. We are terrified of failure. We question our "normality." We see ourself as a poor parent, poor employee, and on the whole, inefficient as a functioning personality. At such times, in our various ways, we begin to bleat for help. . . .

What Is a NORMAL Person?

Whatever it means . . . it does *not* mean an *average* person. Therefore, we can burn about 95 percent of the psychological testing apparatuses. The vast majority of these instruments do nothing more—or less—than measure an individual against a "norm" or an average composite of a given number of subjects. I am strongly tempted to labor this point, but I will pass on with only this notation: I once burdened myself and my clients with massive psychometric diagnostic programs. I found these tests about as helpful as an umbrella with holes. So I've joined the ranks of other therapists of far greater eminence . . . and kicked the habit. I might add that my effectiveness as a healer has not been negatively affected in the least.

I have found no definition of normalcy to be completely adequate. Always, there seems to be a glaring exception to every generalization. This is comforting. I see no reason why there shouldn't be exceptions. In fact, I am genuinely grateful to God that I am cut from different cloth than other people. I walk to my own drumbeat. And to a greater or lesser degree, so does everyone else.

But if I were looking for the lesser of all the many evils which attempt to measure normalcy, this one seems to me to be the most palatable:

The individual who has been adequately affirmed during his developmental years by unselfishly loving, affectionate, mature parents and/or other significant persons can be said to have received the gift of himself. He possesses himself as a man or woman. He knows who he is. He is certain of his identity. He loves himself unselfishly. He is open to all that is good and finds joy in the same. He is able to affirm all of creation, and as an affirmer of all beings is capable of making his fellowman happy and joyful, too. He is largely other-directed. He finds joy in being and doing for others. He finds joy in his loving relationship with his Creator. He can share and give of himself, be a true friend to others, and feel at ease with persons of both sexes. He is capable of finding happiness in marriage or the freely chosen celibate state of life. He is free from psycho-pathological factors which hamper man's free will and is therefore fully responsible—morally and legally—for his actions.

As you can see, this person is what the author refers to as "affirmed." The key point to observe is that such an individual is not incapacitated psychopathologically. While heterosexuality is not stated per se, the intention of it and the implication are patently obvious. We have already made our case for the normalcy of heterosexuality, and it is important to realize that homosexuality is not the *opposite* natural condition.

Homosexuality represents a cross-symbiotic valence relative to heterosexuality. That is, it cannot be accepted as a sexual condition as is heterosexuality; its intensity is completely unrelated to the erotic impulse level of the heterosexual. Homosexuality is a separate entity with its own symbiosis and valence. Its bedfellow is neurosis, of which it is a symptom or expression.

The Failure of Conventional Therapy

One of the strongest reasons responsible for the acceptance of homosexuality as simply an alternative natural form of sexuality, is the widespread failure of conventional psychotherapy to effect a "cure." However, this should not surprise us too much. Conventional psychotherapy is generally ineffective anyway! Be that as it may, the phenomenon of failure has led many professionals to conclude that, since they cannot change it, it must be unchangeable, i.e., endemic and natural—*a normal condition.*

Further, broad studies have been advanced as evidence that homosexuality is a sexual variation within the normal range of psychological functioning (Hooker, 1957). It should be observed, in this regard, that as with biblical scholarship, one can produce what on the surface appears to be the result of thorough academic research—to prove any silly proposition he wishes. An important reason for the preponderance of assorted myths, stereotypes, and unenlightened views of homosexuality which proliferate the body of knowledge is the enormous incompetence and lack of sophistication of behavioral science research. The basic reason for this is presuppositional bias. The size or scope of the study is, more often than not, meaningless.

If it is true that over half of our population has had, at some time in their lives, an actual homosexual experience, and if it is true that 6 to 8 percent of our population is exclusively homosexual—all of their sexual lives—we are talking about twelve to one hundred million plus research subjects to draw upon. Therefore, it is relatively easy to amass a few thousand and impressively support one's viewpoint.

We have already mentioned the church's failure with regard to its ministry to the homosexual community. Now, we note two reactions to this failure. Like the psychoanalytics, the church has on the one hand chosen to accept homosexuality as normal—a pitiful cop-out and evidence of its ineffectiveness; or, on the other hand, to abdicate any responsibility toward the homosexual, taking as its justification the phrase from Romans, "God gave them up unto vile passions . . ."

Can a "Cure" Be Effected?

Most "authorities" and "experts" are beginning to say no. I have been warned by one Christian therapist, a former homosexual, not to speak of homosexuals as being "cured." Presumably, this would alienate present homosexuals who prefer to think that their homosexuality is not a disease. I am most happy to accommodate. Since homosexuality is only a symptom—and I am not interested in curing symptoms—I will simply refer the word *cure* to the underlying neurosis. And neurosis is a disease, albeit in the figurative, not the viral, sense. But this question can be answered in the affirmative if we can answer two other subsidiary questions also in the affirmative:

Have There Been Successful Transitions from Homosexuality to Heterosexuality?

Of course there have.

Dr. Richard Hawes, of the Institute for Reality Therapy, has pointed out that some people can change precipitously, simply by deciding to do so. It is not unknown in penitentiaries around the country for a hardened criminal, with a lifetime history of violence and crime to wake up some morning and say, "To hell with it, I'm not going to do it anymore!" And he doesn't. Hawes, in an expansive mood, further alleges that such precipitous decisions were in accord with Abraham Lincoln's observation that, "You will be as happy as you decide to be."

This may sound so simplistic and naive that one is tempted to dismiss it as the work of a primitive mind. But the truth is, that with certain homosexuals, it happens! When I shared this with one of my psychologist friends, he wouldn't believe it. I told him of a case history. He wouldn't believe it. I told him of another. He still wouldn't believe it. Some people still think the world is flat. Yet it is a fact that countless former homosexuals are so simply because they came to a point in their homosexual life when they decided it was no longer for them. So what happened? They extricated themselves from the life-style, met a girl, fell in love, got married, had kids, and grew old. QED!

Also, while it can be safely said that the psychotherapeutic community is generally unsuccessful in the treatment of homosexuality, it is by no means completely so. Dr. Arthur Janov and his associates have reported substantial success. Dr. Michael Holden, research director for Janov's Primal Institute claims that almost 20 percent of the institutes' clients are homosexual. Not all of them, apparently, desire to be free of their homosexuality, but for those who do, the process seems completely curative. Here is the testimony of one of their patients:

As a lesbian who did come to be cured of it, four and a half years ago, I've been very interested in the answer (Can Primal Therapy Cure Homosexuality?), and, for two and a half of those years, I believed the answer was "yes," based on Primal theory as presented in *The Primal Scream*. Part way through the therapy I changed to "no," based on what I was experiencing in the most intense homosexual relationship I'd ever had, and now, after almost a year of being free of the compulsive need to find a woman who wanted me, I know the answer *is* "yes."[17]

Dr. Kenneth Russell, of Coast Psychiatric Associates, also reports the successful treatment of homosexuality with the application of Gestalt Therapy. The Behavior Modification School, using aversion techniques, also reports success. This is a technique in which the patient is administered a mild shock while being shown erotic photographs of members of the same sex. There is evidence, however, that this technique is not as curative as others. The reason suggested for this is that the modality being used (electric shock or some other aversion stimulus), has a sensate, physiological focus, which can wear off.

The point is, however, that some psychologists, counselors, and the like, do successfully treat the homosexual neurosis. It is utterly absurd to suggest that it is incurable, or to suggest that a homosexual, given proper therapy, cannot become heterosexual. It is true that the patient must desire treatment, which presupposes a personal sense or conviction that his homosexuality is either wrong or intrinsically dysfunctional. But this is true for *any* neurosis and the symptoms thereof.

Every professional, whether medical or psychiatric, knows that you cannot heal anybody who does not want to be healed, unless the means or conditions are available to take this option away from the patient. And even then, with respect to nonmedical pathologies, one cannot psychotherapeutically treat an uncooperative patient. It remains, therefore, for the homosexual to actively seek treatment with the full realization that heterosexuality for him is possible. I believe it to be certain, *in every conceivable, consciously cooperative* case! The only variables would be the therapist involved and the applied therapeutic technique.

It is also important to note that religious faith has been the catalyst to bring many homosexuals into a strong posture of psychospiritual health. One church, Melodyland Christian Center, Anaheim, California, maintains a special Hot Line program, with a staff specifically trained to counsel with homosexual callers. Indeed, the staff are former homosexuals themselves.

It seems the major emphasis in the Christian religious community in coping with the homosexual phenomenon is *conversion.* It is maintained that when a person receives Jesus Christ as Savior and Lord, and receives the gift of the Holy Spirit, his homosexuality either instantaneously evaporates, or he is given the internal strength to pull himself away from it. In either case, the power of God is at work and the Christian cleansed from this sin is often said to have been "delivered."

In some cases, actual freedom from homosexual tendencies does not occur until after a significant period of homosexual abstinence. In other words, while conversion, itself instantaneous, may provide the divine basis for healing, in some cases healing does not follow until later. There can be no question but that it does occur. There are far too many instances of spiritual deliverance from homosexuality to discount.

Troy Perry, our homosexual pastor friend, seems to think that these people are simply suppressing their true sexuality. Many of the Christian homosexuals seem to think that Perry and his associates are simply ignoring the Scriptures. We have already seen that the Christian homosexuals are not ignoring the biblical passages, and we will demonstrate, as well, that "delivered" homosexuals aren't simply suppressing their true sexuality.

We have observed that homosexuals who wish to become heterosexual can do so in one of at least three ways:

1. For some, by simple choice; 2. for others, proper psychotherapy; and 3. still others, by Christian conversion and growth—by divine intervention and deliverance. This leads us to the second and final consideration in our attempt to answer the question, "Can a 'cure' be effected?" No matter how much laying aside of homosexuality is done, or how many claims of healing are made, or what spiritual deliverance occurs, unless we can affirmatively answer the question, "Are these genuine and permanent transitions from homosexuality to heterosexuality?" then we are still stirring the pot. We must accept the challenge that "the proof of the pudding is in the eating."

We must realize in answering this second question that one is not usually successful in willing to forget the past, no matter what the past may be. The charge, "You are willing to *forgive,* but not *forget!*" is not valid. Nobody can forget simply by being willing to do so. Our memory is based on what has been recorded there, not upon our willingness or our ability to recall. Many people cannot consciously recall specific events, but when induced by drugs, or put in a hypnotic or semitrance condition, they recall these events with remarkable clarity.

This being true, it is unfair to expect a former homosexual to *consciously forget* his past. He will remember past homosexual acts in the same way that heterosexuals remember their past. We all remember unpleasant experiences. Further, he/she will remember the pleasure he received. He may or may not actually feel the pleasure with the recollection, but he will be able to recall it all too vividly. But this does not mean that he is still a homosexual any more than a person would still be a criminal simply because he spontaneously recalled past criminal experiences.

The question is, has there been a substantive alteration in subliminal and conscious psychopathology? Dreams and fantasies are important here. Does he still dream and fantasize about members of the same sex, or are his dreams and fantasies heterosexual now? In the subjects I have examined, there has indeed been this subliminal alteration. The time sequence and duration are different in each case, but if a person stays with his decision, his therapy, his faith . . . in time his subliminal homosexual activity will disappear and be replaced by heterosexual activity.

Also, on the conscious level, does the former homosexual have sexual desires directed toward members of the opposite sex? Does he now want to get married; have children; enjoy a family situation? Does he have negative spontaneous reactions to possible homosexual opportunity? Is he still excited sexually by same-sex nudity or warmth? Again, my research has provided evidence that there are thousands of such recovered homosexuals who do not.

Does recurrence happen? For me or anyone to answer that question in the affirmative without qualification would require data from every single former homosexual. This simply is not possible. So I cannot say without qualification that recurrence does not occur. It is possible, however, to generalize fairly. It can be said without qualification that everyone I interviewed felt his homosexual conflicts to be totally resolved. To my knowledge, recurrence has not taken place with any of my former clients. The Primal Institute, who, we recall, declares 20 percent of their clientele to be homosexuals*, reports no recurrence whatsoever. Dr. Janov confidently asserts that those whose neuroses are *cured* through Primal Therapy are cured for as long as they live. EXIT, the very large Melodyland program, reports no recurrence. With these and other available data staring at us, it is certainly fair

* Homosexuals seek help at the institute because of the wide distribution of Dr. Janov's book, *The Primal Scream,* which includes a significant section on the cure of homosexuality.

to say that *most* heterosexuals who profess a homosexual history never go back to it. Thinking about it, that does seem to be a very conservative generalization.

The Nature of the Homosexual Neurosis

Like asthma, hives, headaches, some allergies, assorted aches and pains, overeating, watching excessive TV, alcoholism—which are often psychosomatic—homosexuality is always psychosomatic. Most people think that when you say that something is psychosomatic, you are saying that it doesn't really exist; that it's "all in your head." Not true. Stress is the source of psychosomatic illnesses. Stress produces emotional trauma, anxiety reaction, neurosis, psychosis, ulcers, tics—and homosexuality.

In the case of the homosexual, the stress can be isolated and identified: LOVE! . . . or the lack of it. His need for love has never been adequately met, and given homosexual stimulus and opportunity, he has opted for it—still seeking to be loved. It follows that his need is not sexual, but love-getting. His lack of an adequate love source has produced pain, and with the pain, neurosis and the homosexuality. Ironically, loving a homosexual will not change his sexuality. The damage has already been done. The homosexual may find love, but that will not make him heterosexual. This is so because his original pain—the pain of not being loved adequately—has never been fully resolved.

There is only one kind of love, of which I am aware, that has any genuine and lasting effect upon unresolved neurotic pain, and that is the love of God, and of his Son, Jesus Christ. It is not helpful to talk merely in terms of *agape* and *phileo* (see my book *Love Therapy*, where this is discussed in detail). The pneumapathological character of all neuroses, and for that matter, psychoses, is largely overlooked by the psychiatric community. The fact is, the pneumapathological symbiosis that occurs when the human spirit is nurtured by the Spirit of God *is* congenitally curative.

One may then ask, "Why aren't the Christian homosexuals cured?" The answer to this query is complicated. But I believe it can be answered. 1. The Christian homosexual must reexamine his Christianity. It is possible that he is not a Christian. Before my reader writes this off as being inhumane and cruel, let me remind him that our only substantive rule for faith and practice is the Bible. I think we have demonstrated that the Scriptures teach that God most certainly is not the author nor the sustainer of homosexuality.

It is not unreasonable to assume that a genuine believer would be more sensitive to the weight of biblical evidence. 2. The Christian homosexual may be resisting God's involvement with his sexuality. It is entirely possible that he is withholding his sexuality from God, or is not aware or does not believe that God can and will make him heterosexual; or refuses to believe that God wants to make him heterosexual. 3. The Christian homosexual must cease to ignore sound and obvious hermeneutical principles and assent to the biblical concept that homosexuality is wrong and therefore evil. In short, he must repent. God has never turned anyone away who has come to him in contrition for sin. The psalmist indicates that God loves a broken spirit and a contrite heart. If the person can repent, God will certainly do his part. 4. The Christian homosexual may be *incapable* of allowing God to control his sexuality; and he may be incapable, because of the high valence of his neurosis, of repenting. He may not know how. He must then turn to someone who does know how. There are people who can help him psychotherapeutically and pneumatherapeutically.

These four observations may not provide the answers

for everyone. But they are a good place to begin. Neurotic pain based on the unsatisfied need for love can be resolved with God's love—and so far as I know, only by his love.

Meeting the Need for Love

The therapist's role in helping a client meet his need for love is threefold:

1. He Must Provide Opportunity for Self-love

Most homosexuals, while overtly narcissistic, have a genuine problem with a sense of self-worth. To the homosexual, his narcissism is prima facie evidence of his self-hate. He may talk endlessly about his good looks, his sexual prowess, and attractiveness; but these are all efforts to *convince himself* (he convinces you, which reaffirms himself) that he is a worthwhile person. The fact that he must convince himself of this indicates compensation for an inferior sense of self.

This problem will not disappear until subliminal pain is resolved, the neurosis healed, and the homosexuality gone. A therapist may provide opportunity for this to happen by focusing his efforts on the neurosis and not the homosexuality. He must at least encourage, and I advocate *requiring,* the patient to cease all sexual activity.

Some would disagree with this, suggesting that such a requirement would only increase the valence of the neurosis by overt suppression. In a very real sense, this is precisely what I wish to happen. The more he hurts, the more he will seek relief. The more he feels his pain, the quicker he will respond to therapy. In the meantime, he thinks more of himself for having the courage to refrain from homosexual satiety. Third, the therapist should take every opportunity to reinforce the positive features of his patient's personality. This will assist him in the self-love objective in the same manner as pepper and salt assist in enhancing the flavor of food. Self-love is mandatory. Jesus recognized this fact when he said that we should love our neighbors as we loved ourselves. One must love himself in order to be loved back by himself, i.e., to feel good about himself; have affection and warmth for himself.

2. He Must Provide Opportunity for God's Love

This may seem a ridiculous proposal to a nonreligious therapist. But certainly even he can be intellectually honest enough to admit to the possibility of a personal, loving, caring God. We believers know, of course, that God's love is a fact. Through conscious involvement with God, we have been the recipients of it. We have *felt* it.

And it really isn't all that difficult to provide for this opportunity. All one has to do is structure his therapeutic program to include thoughts about God and allow for emotions to be expressed. The Christian therapist will want to introduce the love of Christ into this program. (More specific information will be provided about this in later pages of this chapter.) But we must provide opportunity for the possible entrance of divine love. It certainly cannot hurt. It can only help. It can bring healing, or at least the beginning of healing.

3. He Must Provide Opportunity for Being Loved by Others

This is more complicated. The therapist must begin with himself. Can he love this homosexual? If he can't, he is beaten before he starts, and he may as well refer the patient to someone else. The therapist is dealing with the basic issue and stress point of his client's problem. If he is going to add to the stress and broaden its scope by failing to love him, he will certainly be doing his client no favor. He had abdicated his role as a healer.

The therapist must impress upon the consciousness of

the patient by persuasion or some other modality, that he is a person worth loving. Again, if the therapist isn't convinced of that himself, he will not succeed. However, it must be said that the actualization of being loved by others probably will not effectively take place until the neurosis is dealt with. But we are concerned with providing opportunity for the end result—not the result itself.

Around these three dimensions of meeting the patient's need for love, the therapist must build or structure his therapeutic program. He should always keep in mind that his client's need is for love. The shedding of his neurosis will open him up for this love.

Therapist/Client Relationship

A certain minimum of qualities must be present in any relationship if it is going to be healthy and productive. What is said here and in the remarks to follow is true whether or not the client is homosexual. The therapist/client relationship and what we wish to achieve in it can be described by one word, *involvement*. The significance of the choice of this word is that it is meant to include a certain mutuality. The therapist will by definition become involved in the processes of his client's problem and hence, his life. In return, the client should feel a mutual attraction to becoming involved in the life of his therapist—with a specific limitation—this is for the client's benefit as well as the therapist's.

That limitation is the walls of the therapist's office; or the specific dimensional latitude of the therapist's *professional* relationship to the client. This does not mean that the therapist should try to maintain an artificial clinical detachment; it does not mean that the therapist cannot be a warm, personable human being. And it does *not* mean that in time, if obvious compatibility exists, client and therapist may become personal and social friends. To me, friendship implies specific obligations, commitments, and responsibilities; such a relationship should be initiated, insofar as possible, free from pathological factors, or professional encumbrances—especially in the counseling field, or anywhere the exchange of funds for services is involved.

As I said, this limitation serves the interests of the client as well. The client should be assured verbally of the total privacy of his relationship with his therapist. He should be assured that under no conceivable circumstances, legal or otherwise, would his case be discussed, alluded to, or even mentioned outside of the office. It will not even be known, unless he reveals it, that he is seeing a therapist. These things are elementary, but they bear strong testimony and support to one of the five ingredients of *involvement:*

1. Trust

Trust is built on the basis of total honesty and candor. The therapist must be willing to be an authentic person if he is to generate trust between himself and his client. By this is meant that he must lay aside all conscious attempts to project a clinical or professional image. Different personalities interpret this differently. It has to do with the arrangement of furniture, seating of client and therapist (in one office I know about, the client is seated in a cushiony sofa built low to the floor, while the therapist is seated in a high-back executive chair which towers over the client, with a broad desk in between—the whole scene giving the therapist the appearance of God), degrees on the wall, the wearing of a white smock, or coat and tie, or an open-necked sportshirt revealing a tanned chest from which glints a golden ankh and chain, or other assorted accoutrements of intimidation. Intimidation, of course, is the name of the game in the minds of some professionals. But it doesn't do a whole lot to firm up genuine trust. Nor does it go very far in the art of healing. Phoniness somehow just isn't all that therapeutic.

2. Interest

Please do not doodle while someone has given you the honor of taking you into his/her confidence. This little rule may seem trifling, but with some clients, doodling, daydreaming, sleeping, playing dead, etc., just isn't all that hard. But if the client picks it up—you are dead as far as your effectiveness is concerned. They want to know, if you'll be so kind, that you are listening.

Therefore, any little comments which indicate that you are on their wavelength are always appropriate: comments such as, "She did what? No kidding! And then what did you do?" Also, facial expressions which indicate interest help, like chuckling at something funny, looking dumbfounded, bewildered, shocked, angry, sad, pathetic, etc. You may smile at these antics, but understand this: if you sit there like a rock, or a computer, or with a contrived clinical expression—you may never see your client again. It is not difficult to show interest if one really is interested.

3. Acceptance

For those heterosexuals who are repulsed by the thought of a homosexual act—not to speak of actually holding a conversation with a homosexual—demonstrating sincere acceptance is a particularly difficult thing to do.

Acceptance may be achieved by development of the ability to distinguish between personal worth and behavior. To my mind, the passage of Scripture which speaks the loudest to Christians about our attitudes toward those whom we might judge or condemn is the narrative on the woman taken in adultery (John 8:1–10). It is a classic illustration of being able to distinguish between personal worth and behavior. The only person involved in this scenario with the credentials (being without sin) to condemn the adulteress (indeed, the biblical responsibility to do so—Lev. 20:10; Deut. 22:22ff.) was Jesus. Instead of accommodating the Mosaic injunction, Jesus said, "Neither do I condemn thee" (personal worth); "Go and sin no more" (behavior). Jesus clearly loved and accepted this woman for what she was—a person of infinite value—but he just as clearly rejected her sin.

You and I must learn to do the same. We do not condone irresponsible behavior simply because we give comfort and acceptance to the individual who is irresponsible. I strongly contend that unless we do this, we will prove to be pitiful counselors indeed.

4. Love

I have argued the point—indeed labored the point—that genuine love cannot exist apart from feeling (affection and anger).[18] Sadly, most expressions of love are more affectation than affection. That is, the act is often unaccompanied by feeling. I refer my reader to my other volume for a detailed discussion of this, but I wish to repeat here that a client must feel that he is loved by the therapist if *involvement* is to be achieved. This means, of course, that the therapist must actually feel the love which he wishes to communicate.

Perhaps this is something that is innate, God-given. But it can also be acquired. It is normal to the healthy individual. In other words, an inability to love simply reflects an inability to unselfishly love one's self, which is neurotic in character. This is why the professional community strongly suggests that any prospective therapist receive therapy himself as a prerequisite to his professional status. If you have problems loving, in particular, those you propose to help, perhaps you should neutralize that inability first.

5. Influence

This "ingredient" of *involvement* is more of a result than a cause. Even so, it is inseparable from the basic concept. As involvement is gained, influence will also muster. By influence is meant that quality necessary to get the client to do what you want him to do. It is that posture of influential control necessary for client response to therapy. Some would call it the ability to manipulate. That depends on what is meant by manipulation. It certainly does not mean to program or otherwise control a patient toward gratification; the process is intended, rather, to be healing in character. The objective is the patient's health and therefore *his* interest.

Without influence, the therapeutic property of the therapist is completely mitigated. What you have is a patient who will resist you at every turn, fight you at each corner, and not respond to any therapeutic technique. He will not allow you into his defense system. Some psychotherapists (both psychologists and psychiatrists) have had patients in therapy for years, and never had influence with them. As a result, years of therapy were wasted, not to speak of the patient's money.

To bring all of this into focus, let me say that a certain chemistry which makes therapy effective must exist between client and therapist. I call it *involvement*. I did not coin it. Dr. William Glasser did with his concept of *Reality Therapy*. But the name, whatever you wish to call it, is not important. Therapy by any name, without the chemistry, produces no catharsis; and without catharsis, there is no healing.

Facilities and Equipment

I do not wish to burden my reader with considerations which are irrelevant to him, but in a few moments I will outline a form of therapeutic procedure which necessitates a few remarks about facilities and equipment. There are three basic aspects of this configuration which I consider essential.

1. Quiet Environment

This is not as easy to come by as one might imagine. In any building there are bumps and footsteps, people talking in the background, toilets flushing, plumbers at work. If it is at all possible, soundproof the room in which therapy will take place. Outside noises can be terribly distracting. Install a plug-in telephone so that it can be unplugged during therapy. Clients who otherwise might release their emotions may hold them in because of the fear of possibly disturbing other occupants in the building. Distractions, or other factors which create tension or exposure, frustrate therapeutic efforts and inhibit the healing process.

2. Furniture

It should be comfortable and arranged in a non-power structure fashion. The therapist should never sit behind a desk during therapy. The reason for this is that it gives the client the impression that his therapist is protecting himself from personal involvement. Large scatter cushions or bean bags are ideal for the appearance of comfort. As we will later discuss, the client will often be lying on the floor, so every care should be taken to make him as comfortable as possible. Overstuffed furniture is excellent, and a sofa is nice.

3. Recording Equipment

Recording each session is of great value: non-therapy hours may be used to reevaluate client response, critique therapeutic technique, and transcribe highly significant periods for minute examination. Recording each session also eliminates the need for copious note-taking, thus freeing the therapist to apply greater concentration to listening and the formulation of crucial questions and comment. Microphones should be in plain view. Never give the client an image of surreptitious motivations.

Length of Session

At issue is the freedom and latitude of not feeling rushed. Frankly, I no longer confine my sessions to fifty minutes. This is especially important and pertinent to the technique to be explained in a moment.

However, even in a simple counseling situation, I give the client enough time to experience some resolution to his problem. Often, one hour is not enough time to do this. Today my sessions are rarely less than one-and-a-half to two hours. Sometimes measurable resolution does not occur until three hours have passed. I have come to sympathize with the client who, undergoing intake procedure when at the end of a fifty-minute session, remarked, "To tell you the truth, Dr. Morris, I feel like you have just stamped me out on an assembly line."

Programmed Cathartic Regeneration (PCR)

The layman will find this segment interesting, but a word of caution is in order here. Psychotherapy is not a game, and it is not something to be attempted without professional supervision. PCR is a therapeutic program which is the result of many hours of study and practice. Professionals are welcome to do with it what they will, but the nonprofessional must content himself to observe from a distance and learn.

I have used and do use other techniques. Counseling, advice, and guidance are often all that is necessary in a given situation. Transactional Analysis is a very good program for family dysfunction. However, the program presented here is focused on the treatment of neurosis (which, you will remember, is the homosexual's specific illness). This technique is also effective in the treatment of psychosis.

What you will see here is a distillation of my own research. It would be wrong to say that it is my concoction. I have borrowed from many therapeutic disciplines. There are some very good psychotherapists practicing today, and I have benefited from their success. In addition, I have supplied my own adaptations, variations, and analyses.

PCR Theory

What I don't understand is, how can a sinful man meet up with a holy God, without either one of them . . . feeling something?—Rev. Jack Hyles

This is a question which has disturbed me also. Intellectually, I know that a person can believe in something, or in Someone, without becoming emotionally affected. Or, at least, I have told myself that. However, deep down, I don't think that I am persuaded. Certainly my own experience with God has been and is a *very emotional* one. But I don't want to be guilty of projecting onto everyone what happens to be a very private personal experience.

Still, the nature of conversion and its subsequent working out in spiritual growth is germane, as I perceive it, to the healing of neurosis. Let me make the point, at the outset, that I equate neurosis and neurotic pain with sin. Not merely personal, self-actuated sin, but also that pain which is caused by being sinned against. It is crucial to realize here that when forgiveness occurs at conversion, and when the burden of sin is lifted, healing takes place at all levels of both conscious and subliminal pain. Healing takes place, but is not completed . . . at least in the vast majority of cases.

What happens to cause the healing can be referred to as a cathartic reaction. With the introduction of the Holy Spirit bearing a new sensitivity to the love of Christ—indeed, overwhelming the individual with the love of Christ—something *is* felt! Release, comfort, love, joy, and all similar adjectives that the mind can conceive may be used to describe what happens when a sinful man meets a holy God. A process is begun which will continue to function as long as the residual pain is exposed to the operative procedures of the Holy Spirit.

This is called regeneration. Theologically this word is used to describe what happens to an individual when the Holy Spirit enters the human psyche, and the individual becomes, in the Pauline vernacular, "a new creature in Christ." In less mystical terms, it simply means that an emotional—but very real—outlet has been discovered for the release of subliminal and conscious pain. Healing has begun.

The word *catharsis* implies an emotional reliving. And in time, with enough such experiences, it is most definitely curative. Most ministers have observed the phenomenon of some Christians "walking the aisle" every time an invitation is given—or almost every time. Some interpret this as getting saved again; others as dedication or rededication of life, etc. What we have missed in our conclusions about this religious quirk is that these people are still having cathartic experiences. Neurotic pain is still in the process of healing. With each new catharsis, a fresh start is generated.

The problem with this phenomenon is that the fundamentalist clerics, not recognizing its value, criticize it and encourage it at the same time. The aisle-walker is told to grow up; that he doesn't have to walk the aisle every time he "feels the Spirit moving." At the same time, the emotional appeals continue, asking people to come, dedicate, rededicate, get saved, go to the mission field, etc. Thus the "inquirer" becomes confused. He stops walking the aisle, stops feeling, and becomes neurotic again.

The solution, of course, is to encourage the believer to "feel" in his relationship to God and let him walk as many aisles as he wishes.

The process of reliving or re-feeling pain is not unique to the religious experience. Many psychotherapists have recognized the curative value of cathartic reactions. Among the most prominent and outspoken is Arthur Janov, author of *The Primal Scream*. Dr. Janov suggests a concept known to him as Primal Pain. In Janovian literature, wherever the word *pain* occurs, it is always capitalized. It always means neurotic pain, an accumulation of pains to formulate Pain—*Primal Pain*. The purpose of his therapeutic procedure, therefore, is to relieve the patient of his Pain through intensely cathartic experiences—what he calls Primals. Often, when his patients experience a Primal scene, they will scream. The effect is almost "electric shock-like" in character. The patient is actually reliving his early childhood Pain. This is not artificial, contrived, or phony (Janov maintains that when it is, it is easily recognizable). If a patient experiences enough of these Primal scenes, he will emerge a new man—a cured man.

The cathartic experience which takes place in Janov's therapeutic procedure is, to my mind, quite similar to that which takes place in religious experience. In the latter, the individual allows God to encounter his pain; in Primal Therapy, the individual reencounters his own Pain. In religious cathartic experience, God feels the believer's Pain; in Primal Therapy, the patient feels his own Pain. I do not wish to argue the comparable effectiveness of either. Suffice it to say that cathartic experience works. An organ will play music just as well in a civic music center as in a cathedral.

A third source from which PCR theory is drawn is called the *Visualization*. This is a labor, really, by which cathartic scenes are precipitated. It is the process of guiding the patient through a completely fictionalized fantasy, and introducing into the fantasy elements which stimulate emotional response. Utilizing the patient's imagination, the therapist causes him to visualize specific scenarios. These could be pastoral and serene, or stormy and violent, or cold, chilling, and with the portent of horror—whatever is necessary to penetrate the patient's defense mechanisms and make him feel. The operative scenarios are suggested and described by the therapist: a confrontation with a deficient parent, a conversation with a patient's hero (Abraham Lincoln, Socrates, Jesus Christ, John F. Kennedy), or a traumatic scene related to his specific neurosis (entering a nest of poisonous reptiles for herpephobia; standing on the ledge of a high building for acrophobia, etc.).

The therapist creates the scene to be visualized, but here input is reduced to a minimum profile. He introduces the patient to the visualization and then leaves the rest up to him. The patient is cautioned not to *try* to create what happens from that point on, but to *allow* whatever spontaneous thoughts that come into his mind to take over. The therapist continues to suggest, guide, and stimulate specific scenes he wishes the patient to experience. He brings in personalities from the patient's past or present—personalities who are significant and exert influence over the patient. He guides the patient into supportive or confrontive situations with these personalities; hugging them, showing affection, anger, hitting them, killing them, raising them to life and killing them again, debating with them, etc.—all designed to precipitate a catharsis.

There are endless possibilities in the formation of new visualizations. Each can be tailored to suit the patient's particular need; or made to focus upon a particular defense, or build up and reinforce an area of emotional weakness.

Programmed Cathartic Regeneration is extrapolated from the foregoing and is, to a large extent, self-explanatory. The specific theory of PCR is based upon the premise that the symbiosis of a God to human encounter produces therapeutic psychopneumalogical catharsis. Presupposed is the reality of God, the love of God, and the healing character of that love. The specific methodology is to bring the human psychopneumalogical quality into direct contact with God, or at least expose it to contact.

It is totally unnecessary for the patient to be a "believer," for this to work. The presuppositions are those held by the therapist—not necessarily the patient. In fact, if the simple mechanics are followed, even the therapist need not be a believer.

The methodology is expressed by *programming,* guiding, and suggesting to the patient specific scenarios which, in his imagination, become real, and which achieve the God/human contact desired. In every case, however, preparation is made through scenarios having nothing to do with interacting with God. Except under unusual and unique circumstances, the patient is never led precipitously from therapist/client interface to client/God interface.

It might be objected that this is all ridiculously artificial. Nothing could be further from the truth. The therapist may outright tell the patient that his "trip" is all in his imagination, that his imagination can do anything it wants, from breathing underwater to riding an insect big as a house from solar system to solar system. So, if in his imagination he encounters God, so what? He is only imaginary. Or is he?

The point is that if, emotionally, the patient encounters the love of God—*he will be affected therapeutically by it!* If he can feel God receive his pain, whether or not he intellectually accepts the idea of God; specific healing takes place. If this happens, his intellect comes under powerful persuasion from his emotions. His emotions tell him that God loves him. It doesn't take long for his intellect to accept it.

Religious trickery? Don't be too quick to judge. Is the reality of God's love legitimate or not? Remember, the therapist makes no attempt to persuade, cajole, or otherwise manipulate the patient to do or believe anything. All he does is create the opportunity for a God/human encounter. The patient's mind and his feelings take it from there.

PCR theory further suggests that once divine love is operative in the neurosis of the patient, each subsequent PCR experience peels away layer after layer of neurotic pain . . . until there is no more pain left. Figuratively, the patient is walking the aisle again and again—each time feeling God operate in his heart. Genuine give-and-take relationship begins to form. The image of God as a loving Father and friend begins to impress itself on the patient's psyche. The scars of past pain (sins) dry up and disappear.

Paul's phrase, "a new creature in Christ" is *inappropriately applied to a new believer,* in my judgment. His pain has not yet been completely resolved. Only if and until every corner of pain has been swept clean will he be, in practice, as well as in faith, truly "born again." Do not misunderstand me. I do not minimize the legitimacy of the initial "conversion" experience. That is real enough and certainly all that is required for forgiveness of sins and eternal life. But it does not completely resolve neurotic pain. It does not wipe away the effects of a lifetime of emotional trauma and dissipation. And once the initial entrance of God into the human psyche occurs, a basis is formed for the therapeutic value of future cathartic experiences, whether religious in character or not.

Therapeutic Format

In this section I wish to outline specific procedure from intake to dismissal. This is provided for the guidance of those professionals who identify with these viewpoints. It should be said that what follows is skeletal. It is impossible and far beyond the scope of this book to include all of the variations and distinctives relevant to this procedure. With this limitation in mind, we begin with:

Intake

Who or by what means a client walks through the door is for the individual therapist or clinic to decide. Some will take only those clients who have been referred by an authority, i.e., police, minister, school system, or other professional. But for most therapists, the client comes on his own or has been referred by a friend. In any case, the first few minutes will be taken in getting acquainted and being friendly. Every attempt should be made to make the client feel at ease; however, small talk should be kept to a minimum. The client is hurting emotionally. He is probably nervous or even frightened and intimidated—before the therapist even opens his mouth.

I have found it beneficial to get the awkwardness of financial considerations over with as soon as possible. So, within fifteen minutes or less, the client usually knows the fees to be charged and how payment is made. After this matter is clarified, the air is clear to proceed to the matters of why the client has come. You can be sure that the financial concerns are paramount to the client. It is best to be crystal clear as to what will be expected. This will avoid later misunderstandings and damage to therapy.

Second, the recording procedure should be explained. This makes some patients nervous. His privacy should be reassured and guaranteed verbally. Information should be provided concerning the value both to the client and to the therapist regarding the recording of the sessions. The microphones should be pointed out and the client reassured that there aren't any more. This may seem silly inasmuch as hidden microphones would be redundant, but say it just the same. A long-playing tape should be used at slow speed to insure no interruption for changing tapes or flipping cassettes. For best results, use reel-to-reel tapes.

Finally, give the client a general explanation of the procedure you plan to use. It is not necessary to be too specific here. Give him just enough information to have something concrete to relate to. Clients become discouraged when they have no sense of direction regarding their therapy. Tell the client that you wish to take him from point A to point B, and outline generally the steps in between. At this point, information about PCR is not necessary.

Problem Orientation

The client has come to you for help. Why? What has brought him here? What, specifically, is troubling him? I usually ask the question, "OK, Jim, can you tell me what is going on?" Just an indirect, noninflammatory question gets the conversation going about his problem. Avoid a superior attitude. For instance, a question such as, "OK, Jim, what's your problem?" is stating the obvious. Further, it places a distance between you and the client. It implies, "The *problem* is yours, not mine, buddy!"

It should be noted here that what he says at this point will probably not be too important, because he will most likely start spouting symptoms. He will begin saying things that are only expressions of a deeper neurosis. But make him feel he has begun in the right direction. Pick up on his comments and try to feel out the neurotic dimensions by noting the symptoms.

He may be like one client of mine and make it easy. In answer to my question, he replied, "I think I'm a homosexual." I relieved him of his doubts. He was a homosexual. The first session should probably end with intake and problem orientation. I use the word *probably* because this is a good jumping off place for the next step, which will take quite some time. These first two steps will take at least an hour in most cases. But let him finish. It is important that a client express his feelings to you. Let him ventilate. It will relieve his surface tension, and you will have taken a major step in gaining his confidence, or *involvement*.

History Taking

Everything you do in future therapy will depend upon how good a history taker you are. History taking is the *key* which unlocks the effectiveness of PCR. What a tape measure and chalk are to a tailor, history taking is to the therapist. The nature and content of your questions, the personalities you will later introduce into PCR, your understanding of the significance of certain events—all depend upon a proper history. The questions are themselves important and must be answered to the fullest.

However, much more information besides the specific answer will be provided. The client will himself raise periphery questions stimulated by the history question. Furthermore, he will answer all of these questions for you, completely unprompted.

Take as many notes as you can—but make absolutely

certain the recorder is in good working condition. This is one session for which transcription is a must. As he answers each question, let him talk until he can say no more, and then ask, "Is there anything else?" If the answer is no, move on to the next question. Here are the questions:

What is your educational history? This question will provide information about the character of the formative and growing-up years. Ask additional questions about favorite teachers, professors, good, bad, etc. This information will include how many schools he attended and how many times he moved as a child, and many other items relevant to later therapy.

What is your employment background? Ask about his military service. Did he like it? Does he get along well with employers, etc.?

What is your religious background? Don't let this question drop with an answer such as, "I don't have any." What about parents? Grandparents? Anyone who imposed religious viewpoints on him or otherwise influenced him religiously. Get him to explain his relationship to God if he admits to one. Milk him dry for any reference point to be used in later therapy.

Describe all you remember about your romantic heterosexual relationships. Get him to go all the way back to childhood sweethearts. Any childhood experimentation? Masturbation? Past and present sexual activity? Did he ever go steady? Engaged? Married? Divorced? Have him name every girl he can remember that he loved or was infatuated with.

Describe your present emotional climate. Let him talk and say anything he wants. Get him to talk about his feelings. Tell him not to intellectualize his feelings, i.e., "I think I'm a very happy person." You are not really interested in his evaluation. You are interested in his feelings: I am happy. I am upset. I am frightened, etc.

TREATMENT

List as many major traumas in your life as you can.
Every one of these will provide at least one scenario for
future cathartic possibilities. Get him to describe them—
though not in too much detail. Note his feelings while
talking about them. On which ones does he sigh? Choke
up? Tighten his lips? Display facial tics? Weep outright?
Save this as vital information for later. Note the ones
he does *not* list and compare with the information received during the intake.

Who are the most significant people to you now? Ask
about people he's presently living with, and with whom
he has contact. These will include family, friends, working
associates. Ask him to describe the relationships.

Who has influenced you the most during your lifetime?
Answers to this and the previous question may be the
same in certain instances—all provide material for later.

Describe your relationships with: (pick out any number
of significant others previously mentioned you deem
relevant.)

*Describe some specific childhood incidents which were
not traumatic.* This should give you some insight into
the things that provide pleasure for your client. These
will be the things that also feed his ego and will tip off
his evaluation of himself.

After the history has been taken and transcribed, study
it carefully. Mark it with a colored pen and prepare your
PCR scenarios from it. Taking the history will rarely take
less than two hours and it should provide you with enough
information to make conclusions about the nature and
personality of your client and the direction therapy will
take. The answers to the above questions are more valuable to me than any battery of psychometric evaluations.

Initiate PCR

If your analysis indicates psychoneurotic pathology, prepare your first PCR process for the next session. This

will be your third encounter with your client, and by now you should have spent some three to five hours with him. After he is seated, explain to him the basic procedure and theory. Tell him that it is vital that he relax during the program, and to avoid *trying* to create scenarios. Instruct him to let you do that. All you want to know are the thoughts that come to him during the scene. He is to tell you of his feelings. When you instruct him to speak to someone, he is to do it verbally. He must allow his feelings to take over and must not suppress them.

After the explanation, provide him a comfortable place to lie down, and tell him to get as comfortable as he can. Turn the lighting down, so that it is not dark but subdued. Tell him to spread his legs (creating a sense of vulnerability), and to place his hands by his side (not crossed, or holding onto each other, or any other way). Tell him to open his mouth and breathe deeply. Have him inhale; exhale slowly; inhale again, filling his lungs to capacity; then exhale slowly. Ask him to repeat this five to ten times. Now tell him to relax as completely as possible.

By this time you are speaking slowly, softly, but with clarity and definition. To generate further relaxation, say to the client, "Jim, I am going to count from 100 backwards to zero. I want you to focus your mind on each number as I count." Beginning with 100, count backwards, slowly, deliberately. In order to arrest concentration, reverse the progression three to four times. For example, ". . . 87 . . . 86 . . . 85 . . . 85 . . . 85 . . . 86 . . . 87 . . . 88 . . . 89 . . . 88 . . . 87 . . . 86 . . . 85 . . . 84," and continue on. Beginning with *20,* watch the second hand on your watch. From 20 to 15, at least five seconds is allowed to pass between each number. From 15 to 10—ten seconds; from 10 to 5, fifteen seconds; from 5 to 0, thirty seconds. By the time the counting has ceased the patient's tension level should be light years away from that which he had when he came into the office.

This process will be repeated with each session of PCR. However, you will find that you will not have to begin with 100 very often in the future. Once the patient gets the point of the exercise, his relaxation will come much quicker. You may wish to begin with 75 the next time, perhaps 50 the next, and so on.

But we are not done with relaxation. In addition, the patient must become aware of himself, aware of his own body and personality. At this point he is asked to concentrate on some extremity of his body—perhaps the little toe of his left foot. From this point the therapist guides the patient in the awareness and relaxation of each section of his body; beginning with the foot, the ankle, calf, knee, thigh, hips, abdomen, stomach, chest, shoulders, upper arm, forearm, hands, fingers, neck, head, facial hair, facial features, clothes, cushion pressure, external sounds, internal sounds, etc.

We are now ready for the first cathartic scenario. Ask the patient to imagine himself drifting away from his body. Have him stand next to his body and observe himself on the floor. Have him imagine an opening somewhere in his head through which he can enter his own brain (mind). Tell him that he has entered a room in his own mind. He alone knows the dimensions of that room, how large, the furnishings, windows, carpeting, etc. At this point, turn the scenario over to him and have him describe to you the nature of the room and everything in it. It is dirty or clean? Dark or light?

On rare occasions, the patient will not be able to imagine what you are suggesting. He may not be able, because of defense mechanisms, to imagine himself standing inside a room inside his own head. If he cannot, after continued suggestions and alterations, move on to another scenario. In my experience this has never happened. But one must be prepared for the theoretical possibility.

The effect of this exercise is to get the patient in touch with himself as a real entity. After the descriptions have been exhausted, suggest a spot or stain on the floor or walls of the room. Ask him to get some soap and water, or a fire hose, or spot remover, and clean the spot. Sometimes the spot will not go away. Sometimes the spot is a bloodstain. This is highly significant. It indicates a subliminal attitude of helplessness and despair, or of guilt. Later, this spot will be influenced by the introduction of Christ and his cleansing love.

The introduction of a significant other is often appropriate at this time. Tell the patient to invite someone important to him (or someone you suggest) into the room with him. Stimulate a conversation between the client and this person, possibly for a confrontation. Have the client speak *not to you,* but to the person he is confronting. You may suggest certain attitudes for the client to assume. You may tell the client to hug, kiss, argue with, or tell this person off.

If the client begins to feel or show signs of emotional involvement, suggest that he breathe deeply and allow the feeling to come. Tell him to let the feeling take over. It makes no difference what the feeling is: anger, hatred, fear, grief, sorrow, joy, happiness, ecstasy. It is important that he feel it completely. His actions may become involuntary, orgasmic. If he begins to thrash about, cry, or scream—anything short of injuring himself—let it happen. It will pass in a few moments. The catharsis is always therapeutic because he is resolving pain.

However, these things may not happen. They probably won't in the first session or two. Be prepared with a series of scenarios through which the patient will be guided. At the point at which you consider it the most fitting, introduce this scenario:

Jim, imagine yourself in a crowd of people. You are on
the side of a hill and the people are moving up the hill.
Some of them seem very angry, others are obviously grief-
stricken. Most simply seem to be curious. You join the
crowd and make your way up the hill. You hear weeping
and moaning. You make your way higher and higher
and the hill takes on an unusual shape. There are two
cave openings side by side. They resemble eyes. In fact,
the whole hill resembles a misshapen human skull. At
the top of the hill you come to a stop. Before you is a
large cross. There is a man on the cross. A wreath of
long thorns is pressed down on his head. He is fastened
to the cross by spikes driven through his hands and feet.
There is a large wound in his right side. You become
aware now that you are completely alone with the cross
and this man. He is alive. You see him shift his weight.
The flies licking at his blood fly away for an instant and
return. His eyes are opening. He looks at you. His mouth
is trembling. He is trying to speak. Finally, with great
effort he speaks to you . . . listen carefully. It is barely
above a whisper. What does he say to you, Jim?

I have had some beautiful answers to this question. Answers such as "He can't talk. All he can do is cry. He's
crying for me"; "He says, 'I've been waiting for
you . . .' "; "He says, 'I love you. . . .' " Some people reject this scene altogether, only to be haunted by it when
they leave. I may get a phone call later telling me that
Jesus finally got through to them.

Therapy continues in this fashion, session after session;
each session lasting a minimum of two hours. After each
PCR session, discussion should be held with the patient
regarding his feelings, his own interpretations, and in-
sights gained. This is continued until and when cathartic
experiences seem to be slackening. This is an indication
that healing is taking place, that neurotic pain is subsid-
ing and being resolved. With the resolution of neurosis
comes emotional health and the ability to evaluate previous symptoms with objectivity. And the realization dawns
that whole habits of life and overpowering proclivities
no longer hold them in abject slavery. Homosexual symp-

toms and feelings subside with each catharsis, followed by the conscious decision to kick the homosexual traces entirely, with the person in possession of the full capability of inner power to successfully carry it off.

When measurable healing becomes obvious; when the patient is well on his way to emotional health, it is time to refer him to a *group*. If a patient is seen once a week for a two- to three-hour session, one-to-one therapy will average three to four months. This is by no means an inflexible guide. The only legitimate guide is the intensity of cathartic scenes, their frequency, and the specific areas covered (indicated by the history).

Do not be deceived by plateaus. A highly cathartic patient may walk in one day and be completely nonresponsive. This does not mean that he is well. Healing is determined by the pattern and nature of cathartic experiences. But there will come a time when he will no longer need to "walk the aisle," when he feels secure enough in himself and his relationship to God (however that is extrapolated from these experiences), that he will no longer need individual therapeutic attention.

Group Therapy

After two months of PCR, the therapist will begin to notice definite signs of healing—sometimes even before two months. When a certain "momentum" is observed in this regard, it may be time to refer the client to a group. It is a "judgment call," as the sporting world likes to say, but the therapist must make this decision whenever he feels the time is right.

PCR in group therapy is conducted in precisely the same manner as with an individual. There must be plenty of room to accommodate the group, however. The therapeutic program focuses on the expertise of the therapist. He conducts and guides the scenarios, asks the questions, makes the suggestions. The participants are instructed to talk to the various significant others (be they persons, animals, or God), in silence. Feelings are allowed to be expressed freely. After the actual PCR session, open discussion is held. All of the participants are allowed to speak. The others have the opportunity then to observe the subliminal activity of their counterparts and are permitted to make analyses and suggestions themselves.

Group sessions last from three to five hours each and the individual patient should continue until both he and the therapist agree that he should leave. He should be allowed to continue as long as he wishes, but he shouldn't quit these weekly group sessions against the advice of the therapist. He should be allowed to return, after his therapy is completed, as often as he desires, so long as previous arrangements have been made with the therapist. Dismissal occurs usually within six months of regular participation in group therapy. Sometimes, however, the patient may wish to stay with it for years—even a lifetime.

The Relevance of Deep Breathing

It is easy to observe the respiratory functions in everyday life. Whenever we sigh, we are releasing tension. When we cry, our respiration system often produces involuntary sobs, or spasms of inhaling and exhaling. Watch the heaving, jerking chests of sobbing children. Breathing is constantly associated with our emotional climate. We gasp when startled. Deep, nervous breathing indicates excitability. Shallow breathing prevents the egress of neurotic pain.

This is why deep breathing is so important in PCR. When one begins to feel, I often encourage him to open his mouth wide and breathe deeply. I tell him to pull the feeling from below his stomach, to allow his feelings to come out as he exhales. There is no need to be concerned about hyperventilation. The egress of neurotic pain usually does not produce hyperventilation in the classic sense, no matter how spectacular it may appear. Even if problematic hyperventilation were to occur, it can be controlled easily enough.

Preparation Against Defenses

If a client is not *emotionally* uncomfortable, it will be difficult to penetrate his defense systems. If, in PCR, I get "shut down" every time an emotional threshold is approached, the chances are good that the patient's defenses have not been sufficiently weakened. Sometimes in therapy a patient may be beginning to breathe deeply, tears begin to form, and then all of a sudden he involuntarily pushes his "shut down" button, and you are back where you started.

This can often be avoided by employing certain mechanisms prior to therapy. Have the patient skip the meal he would normally eat prior to therapy. He comes to therapy hungry. Have him skip two meals if necessary. If this does not work, have him stay up late the night before and get up early that morning, or stay up all night. The severest measure would have him up all night, alone, with no television, no telephone, no writing materials, no reading materials, no alcohol or tobacco, no food—just himself—and maybe some music. He will come to you the next day in a substantially weakened condition.

Prevention

Nowhere is the proverb, "An ounce of prevention is worth a pound of cure," more poignant than in the field of psychotherapy and spiritual welfare. Specifically, what can a parent do to prevent his child from becoming a homosexual?

The first thing that should be said is that there are no guarantees. It is impossible in a world of obscenity and terror to shield a child from all exposure to trauma. But there are at least three things that will substantially lessen your child's possibility of becoming homosexual.

1. Love and Tenderness

During pregnancy, take great pains to get proper rest and eat right. It goes without saying to avoid all forms of drug abuse and alcohol abuse. Live life in a low profile. Try not to argue, fight, or otherwise get into high tension situations. Exercise as strenuously as your doctor will permit.

During the first three months of your baby's life, be especially attentive to his needs. *Do not leave him crying in the crib* during this time. Avoid loud noises and other assorted traumatic situations. Do not insist on training your child to "sleep through the night" for these three months. If it happens naturally, fine. But do not force it. Hold him a lot. Hug and kiss him a lot. Love him a lot. Play with him a lot. If you must argue with your spouse, do it where the baby can't hear it. I cannot stress enough the importance of shielding your baby from stress during these first months of life.

As he grows, do not rush potty training. Allow development to occur as naturally as possible. If discipline is called for, by all means impose it. But discipline must be balanced with loving attention. Heap love upon your child. Don't worry, you won't give him too much. Express it in ways that are substantially meaningful—not by buying him everything he wants, or giving him a lot of bright, expensive goodies. As your child develops, make it your goal to provide him with a strong image of self, and a *strong feeling* of being accepted and loved by his parents.

2. Provide Opportunity for God's Love

This does not mean church nurseries, but certainly church is included. One important point needs to be made here: the chances are very good that if your child is not having his need for love met by his parents, it will be a long time—if ever—before his need will be met by God. A child will know that the love of God can be felt because you have provided him with a precedent.

Provide a loving God/human atmosphere in the home. This does not mean a family altar, or grace at meals, or Bible readings, or bedtime prayers; but it may include all of these. Religious activities in the home are valuable only if they are not banal and ritualistic. They must not be considered as ends in themselves. How the children are treated; how love is expressed in the home, spontaneous talk about the Lord, touching each other; "touching" God; all of these are much more impressive to the mind of a child than church activities.

3. Role Modeling

Provide the child with a loving, strong, same-sex model to identify with; also, a strong opposite-sex model. In other words, a child needs to see in pragmatic life experience the extension of his own heterosexual sexuality. His heterosexuality is not necessarily reinforced, but a subliminal aversion to the unnaturalness of homosexuality will be prompted when confronted by homosexual stimuli. The "unisex" phenomenon has contributed much toward the confusion of human sexuality, in my opinion. If, as we grow in our learning experiences, we encounter data that runs counter to the natural order, confusion and blurring of definition may occur. So a father should provide a positive male image, and mother a positive female image.

CHAPTER SIX

TRANSSEXUALISM

To say that transsexualism is a controversial and volatile issue in our society today is to understate the case. Transsexuals are popping up in all of the usual crucibles of controversy, namely, the radio-TV talk shows, and the gossip-oriented, astrology-crowded, three-ring-circus tabloids. It all began with a young man who in 1952, recently discharged from the military, walked into his doctor's office and declared that he wanted to change his sex. A few months later Christine Jorgensen emerged as the world's first male to female transsexual.

For the next decade the numbers of men requesting a sex change began to rise dramatically. However, American physicians were still leery. A few were willing to provide estrogenic hormones preparatory to surgery, but the operations were performed in other countries—primarily Morocco. Some fifteen years later, U.S. hospitals began performing similar surgery on persons "unable" to live in the sex role expected of them by virtue of their anatomy.

Nearly all of the requests for sex change came from men. The ratio of men to women requesting the change is about three to one. The reasons postulated for this numerical inequality are highly speculative and theoretical. Some suggest the reason is *psychodynamic;* that is, the first and most significant other person a baby comes into contact with is his mother. It is, therefore, theorized that a male must disidentify himself with his mother in order to develop his masculinity. Girls, obviously, do not have to do this.

A second postulation is *sociological* in character; that is, society provides greater latitude for females to express their sexuality. It is easier, they reason, to live life as a female. One can wear pants or a dress, live with other women, and engage in romantic relationships with less agitation from society and less need for approval.

Others suggest the reason to be *neuroendocrinological.* Man, they say, is, in his basic mammalian state, anatomically a female. This is due to the fact that male hormones must be supplied by the mother to the male fetus while this is not true for the female fetus (Jost, 1947). Thus it is much more logical for a man to desire to become a woman than the other way around. Anybody can see that. Finally, surgery is simply *more practical.* It is surgically much simpler to perform a penectomy and castration, and construct a vaginal opening, than it is to construct a penis! Soon, however, with the mushrooming faddism of transsexualism, it would not surprise me to see "genital banks" cropping up in hospitals around the country.

If I seem less than sympathetic to the transsexual phenomenon, perhaps you will better understand when we examine the basic motivations for the sex change surgery. This is a primary concern for doctors. In their commitment to the hippocratic oath, they must be absolutely certain that this surgery will, indeed, be therapeutic. The primary concern is the nature of the prognosis. Will this person be a successful contrasex personality? Is he suffering from his present sexual identity and will irreversible surgery help him or will he live to regret it?

Most surgeons who perform this surgery are quite sincere in their attempts to answer these questions adequately. They wish to be healers—not destroyers. Besides, an unhappy patient who inconveniently decides he wants his penis back, might also decide to sue for malpractice! Understandably, every effort is made to insure against that possibility.

1. Misfit Males
These are people who are not necessarily feminine, but who are sociopathological misfits. They never seem to fit into the mainstream of society. They reason that they can only be happy if they are allowed to live as women.

Homosexual incidence is high with this group, as is criminal proclivity.

2. Psychosis

This, in my opinion, is the major reason that people not only desire, but go through with sex-change surgery. Only a delusionary state of mind would permit this kind of mutilation. Many of these people's delusions are so strong that they actually bleed cyclically—from the anal canal and through the urethra. They actually think they are women. Of course, the delusion does not have to be *that* strong to precipitate surgery.

Such a man may not believe he is a woman, *ipso facto,* but to some measurable degree, he does think he is. And of course, after surgery is completed, he must believe it if for no other reason than emotional justification.

I am fascinated by psychiatrists who are often just as deluded as their patients. A well-known West Coast psychiatrist vehemently maintains that a person who is anatomically and chromosomally a male (or female, as the case may be), may be born with a *female mind;* and that when surgery is performed, "to align their bodies with their mind," you have a *de facto* woman! This is sheer illusion. This doctor, and those like him, are indulging in nothing more than mystical, psychiatric guruism. It is interesting to note that most surgeons will refrain from performing sex-change surgery if they suspect psychosis. They are disturbed perhaps by one thought: "What if this patient wakes up one morning and discovers his psychosis is gone?"

3. Effeminate Homosexuals

Not all homosexuals are obviously effeminate, but many are. (It should be noted that there are many "effeminate" *heterosexuals* as well. One does not become homosexual, necessarily, because his bone structure is small, his body is hairless, and his skin is soft.) However, those effeminate homosexuals who are oppressed by society and guilt-ridden about their sexual diversion may request a sex change. The medical community, once again, does not consider these people good prospects for sex change. They still have a male identity instead of a "female identity." The latter, of course, would by definition, be psychotic.

4. Transvestites

As we have already mentioned, these are (exclusively) men who cross-dress for erotic reasons. Women do not do this. If this becomes a pattern of life and they are successful in "passing" as a woman, they become less erotic as the comfort level of living in this way rises. If their adopted life-style becomes so impressed on their minds that they are actually uncomfortable dressing as men, and if they are living their lives as women, they may desire a sex change. The prognosis for surgical and permanent change for this group is better, but is still held to be suspect by many physicians, due to fetishism.

5. Males Who Identify Themselves as Females

These, prognostically, are the best candidates for sex change surgery. These are people who from their earliest childhood were femininely identified and behaved like girls. They enjoyed playing with dolls and dressing like girls, and associated primarily with a female peer group. Many consider it a sophisticated child-rearing philosophy not only to allow, but to encourage little boys to play with dolls. I wonder how many parents would encourage this if they knew that they were priming their son for a possible sex change later in life. I want to emphasize that boys, who, early in life, are psychologically reinforced with feminine role qualities *are the most likely prospects for surgical sex change.*

How are these prospects screened for possible surgery?

It is interesting to note that clinical emphasis has shifted from an evaluation of the past to an evaluation of the present and future. They wish for a patient to prove that he can function better socially as a female. "Dress all day, every day in the role you desire. Get a job in that role. Move to a new neighborhood and start a new life in that role. You don't need immediate surgery to really know what it's like." Often, the surgeon will supply the patient with the relevant hormones (injected or taken orally) to assist in his new roleplaying.

One reaction of the hormone estrogen given to a male will be decreased sex drive and impotence. A rather pragmatic medical logic becomes operative here. It is better, they reason, to experience this loss chemically at first, as it were, on a trial basis. Later, if no problem comes, surgery can be performed. Breast growth will begin, and will help psychologically to support the patient's "passing" role. It encourages the patient to know that female hormones are circulating in his bloodstream. The skin becomes softer, and more feminine characteristics develop. Something must be done, however, about the hair. Those preparing for sex change often go through the costly program of facial hair epilation at this time. Estrogen is also ineffective for raising the male voice to a more feminine level.

However, androgen or testosterone enanthate will lower the female voice to a male level. Androgen will also promote facial hair growth. Considerable growth of the clitoris will take place. The sex drive will increase, menstruation will cease, and general body hair will grow.

No matter how compelling the pathos may sound, coming from those quarters that are pleading for social acceptance for the surgical procedure, we should not hide our faces to the blatant artificiality of it. Sex change surgery is totally, completely cosmetic in substance and character. It is not even very good cosmetics. Doctors do not affix a penis onto a female transsexual. They affix a *prosthesis*. It is a pitiful substitute—even in appearances. It bears only remote resemblance to an actual penis and no surgical effort is made with regard to constructing a scrotum. It has little, if any, sexual value. The circumstances are little better for the castrated and penectomied male. Vulva and vagina construction cannot be placed in the same context with the natural product. The sex drive diminishes substantially with castration for the male, and orgasm may never again occur. Orgasmic activity is retarded for the female also.

The most important consideration for these patients is their mental state. If they were born anatomically one sex or the other, no amount of surgery will change that. The surgery should be psychotherapeutic, not physiological. Actual genital change only worsens the psychosis. Unlike the aforementioned psychiatrist, I maintain that the mind should be brought back into alignment with the body, rather than the other way around. It should be noted that the latter is a physiological impossibility, anyway. A man is not provided with a uterus or ovaries; a woman is not provided with gonads or sperm or a scrotum. Reproduction and other normal sexual functions of the genitals are forever impossible after surgery. The possibilities of mental healing exceed by light-years the possibility of physiological realignment.

Is a transsexual the same thing as a homosexual? The answer to that question is not simplistic. Some would have us believe that he is not—in no uncertain terms. They may be right. If the patient identifies himself mentally and emotionally as a woman, he is not homosexual; he is psychotic. He has departed from reality. He is not a woman, but he believes and acts as though he is. We must remember that homosexuality is not a condition. It is a symptom of neurosis, or neurotic pain.

If, however, the transsexual is not suffering the delu-

sion that he is a woman (or *vice versa*), and his desire
"to be a woman" is based upon his erotic attraction for
men, then by definition he is homosexual. The difference
may be subtle, but it is, nonetheless, substantial. Either
case, it is important to point out, will respond to adequate
therapy.

A problem of substantially different character is that of
anatomically intersexed infants. At birth, such a baby
is constructed so that it is impossible to determine, on
genital examination, whether it is a boy or a girl. Or,
as in most cases of intersexed infants, the child is chromosomally a male (or female), hormonally a male, but with
female external genitals. The reverse would be true for
a female. These are the extremes. Existing between are
the various degrees of hermaphroditic (morphodite)
conditions.

When such births occur, it becomes the responsibility
of the medical community to decide which sex the child
will be. This decision is based primarily on the gender
dominance or larger evidence of the external genitals.
If a genetic female is born with male genitals, the child
is assigned the sex of a boy. (Homosexual incidence among
the intersexed is extremely rare, as is bisexuality. Affirm-
ation of sex identity is a sore point with the parents,
and conscious effort is made to clarify it.) Bear in mind
that this decision is based wholly on biological evidence.
The genetic structure of a person is just as much a part
of his body as is a penis, or vagina, or for that matter,
an arm or a leg. There is nothing mystical about genes.

Prior to the third month of pregnancy, the sexual organs in male and female fetuses, both internal and external, are identical. However, they have differing genetic
makeup. The same genetic influence that makes eyes blue
or hair brown also determines maleness or femaleness.
But occasionally a gene or genes may be defective or func-

tion in a disharmonic fashion. When this happens, congenital irregularities occur. Sometimes this will result in an intersexed infant. It is physically impossible to realign the discordant correlation of genetic, hormonal, and genital dysfunction. However, if the situation is hormonally corrected, puberty will usually confirm the dominant genital preference. But not always.

For example, if a genetically established female is born with an atrophied penis of the microphallic type (a small tubular appendage with substantially diminished glands), and undescended testes, the doctor will surgically remove the penis and testes, and the child will be raised as a girl. The atrophy is simply too severe. The testes will not descend even with the release of androgen at puberty, and could pose a pathological threat to the child. Her reproduction capability will depend entirely on hormonal therapy and the presence and integrity of internal reproductive organs. She will be capable, in most cases, of orgasm and penile insertion.

What has happened here? Simply this: the child has become a surgically altered transsexual. She will grow up and function as a girl, although she will be quite aware of the different nature of her anatomy when, later in life, she compares herself with other girls.

But suppose, as is the case with many such intersexed infants, the child grows up and the discovery is made that the doctors have made a mistake in sex assignment? Suppose in the case just mentioned, the medical decision (hopefully always with parental approval and support) was *not* to remove the penis and testicles? The child is now an adult male. His penis has not been affected by hormonal influence, his testicles still remain undescended. The enormous psychological stress of derision by his male peers, his inability to function sexually, his constant identity confusion, have led him to seek the surgical procedure that he should have had at birth. Daniel becomes Danielle. He is now a she . . . and a transsexual.

It is ridiculous to surmise why God would permit such a "mistake of nature" as an anatomically intersexed infant. I will not attempt to discuss the origins of the soul here; but one thing is for certain; the determinism of God is most certainly passive, or based on his knowledge of what will happen anyway, when it comes to the outworking of the natural order as he himself established it. Unless it is true with the noncorporeal part of man, there is no new creative act on God's part when a human being is conceived. We are the products of the lovemaking of our parents, whether baby-making was the intention or not. We carry the genes of our parents because of the physiology of natural processes. God did not "make" a sexually intersexed infant. He is that way because of the conjoint genetic differential of his parents.

Such a person deserves our warmest support, love, and acceptance. He cannot help what he/she is any more than another can help having blue eyes or brown hair, or needing to have his eyesight corrected with special lenses, or needing a toupee for baldness.

CHAPTER SEVEN

HOMOSEXUALITY & CHILDREN

Michael's parents were gone, and the house on Third Avenue was empty. It was a balmy Georgia afternoon and the sun filtered softly through the sheer white curtains. Beneath the windows on the sofa lay Tony, his pants and underwear pulled down around his knees. Michael was on his knees beside the sofa. He was crying. Around Michael stood Larry, Howard, Gene, and me. We were all much bigger than he, and it was the threat of being beaten that had put Michael where he was right now.

Tony was the bully of the block. He could beat us all up—or so we thought. The idea of experimenting sexually with Michael was his idea. The rest of us went along with it simply because Tony thought it would be really great.

It was easy for the four of us to grab and hold Michael. He gave up and cried easily. It was doubly easy because his eyes were crossed and he wore thick corrective glasses which only made him look worse. When he realized what was going to happen, he panicked.

About this time, my conscience began to get restless. I didn't really want us to do this to Mike. After all, we did play together a lot. But I didn't want to attract Tony's anger, and the other boys were more Tony's friends than they were mine. Mike looked at me. He felt, I thought, that I was betraying him. I began to weaken.

Mike struggled against Howard and Larry who were holding him. It was no use. They pulled him down to his knees and Tony forced himself on the smaller boy.

That was all I could take. I knew if I stayed any longer I would throw up. I was standing next to the door, which was closed. Before anyone knew what I was doing, I was out of the door and running up the street to my house.

I didn't look back. I ran all the way home, into the house, through the living room and into my bed. I covered my head with the covers and cried.

I was nine years old.

The first thing the reader should realize is that the above related experience, though true, was not an act performed by homosexuals. None of us were, Mike least of all. The whole thing was a bizarre adventure, like Huck Finn's excursion on the Mississippi, or Tom Sawyer and Becky Thatcher in a cave together. Unfortunately, however, it is an example of how children first begin to discover their sexuality. The primary motivation in children's discovery of sexuality is fun and adventure—not sex, or love. Little boys showing off their penises to one another or pulling down their pants in front of their little neighborhood female friends is not sick—it is simply evidence of a lack of loving sexual education given at home.

So far as I know, none of the boys described in the above scene grew up to be homosexuals. Michael grew up and joined the marines, which I interpret as an expression of his search for a stronger masculine image. The point of relating this to my readers is to illustrate that children are indeed aware of homosexuality. They know about homosexual acts. But to say that this kind of experimentation is psychologically harmless, is utterly absurd. If, for example, a child was undergoing love-source stress, and if the proper chemistry and ingredients of emotions and experience were in process, then such an experience could very well have been a *bona fide* homosexual act. It would, to say the least, have reinforced other emotional and experiential conditions in the neurosis of the child. It would have contributed positively to that child actually becoming a homosexual.

It is alleged by some psychologists, among them the noted Dr. Joyce Brothers, that homosexual teachers would have no effect upon children and their possible development into homosexuals (the Merv Griffin show, 7/28/77). This is transparently untrue. *Any* homosexual stimuli will contribute to homosexual acting-out. If a teacher lives in an open homosexual relationship, the students will most certainly be aware of it. Students are affected by a teacher either positively or negatively. Some will love him, admire, him, and even wish to emulate him. If the student holds this popular attitude toward the teacher, the teacher's influence valence is extremely high. And a student who, because of neurotic stress already discussed, is susceptible to homosexual stimuli, most certainly will be affected by the homosexuality of his teacher.

Parents, however, should not become unduly alarmed if they discover that their child has become involved in homosexual experimentation. The matter should be discussed calmly and with understanding and love. Almost all children are going to experiment with their sexuality. This includes playing doctor, behind-the-bushes exhibitionism, masturbation, homosexual experimentation, actual sexual intercourse, and fondling. It is the wise parent who does not become unglued when something like this happens. But it is not wise to ignore it. Open discussion within the family about sex and sexuality is probably the healthiest preventive against sexual dysfunction in later life, including homosexuality. Privacy of sexual expression can be discussed without emphasis upon secrecy and furtiveness.

Children should be told about homosexuality and the homosexual world in these family discussions. It is a major psychological tragedy that sex, let alone homosexuality, is rarely intelligently and sensitively talked about in the home. Children are left to learn about it on the street and playground. If you do have the courage to broach this subject with your children, may I suggest that you not be too pious about it. They should be told what God thinks about homosexuality, and they should be told that God created the sexual impulse for the pleasure of his children. They should be informed that its primary function is to express love and not merely for self-gratification. But do not invoke the wrath of God in the sexuality context.

Suppose you have a child like Michael, who has gone through what may have been for him a very severe homosexual trauma? Or suppose it was worse? We all are quite aware of the lurid events that occur around the country. No child is really exempt from this sort of thing. It happens, no matter how much we try to protect and shield our kids from it. It is best to be prepared.

When should your child be told about homosexuality? It really varies. It depends on the intellectual sophistication of your family and the emotional climate of the child's mind. Only the parent is really in the position to make such a judgment. Generally speaking, however, any child old enough to understand ethical concepts, and mature enough to absorb the data without undue emotional response, should be provided the information.

If your child is homosexually molested, or for that matter, sexually molested in any fashion, it is absolutely crucial that the parent not panic or react violently. Your child is desperately in need of comfort and tenderness at such a time. The more of a conflagration that is made over such an incident, the greater an impression of terror will be made on the child.

If the child is upset, quizzing him about all the ugly details at that time is also damaging. If information is needed for the authorities, it is best for the parents to provide it, if possible. Questioning should be done at a time when everyone is calm, and in a mature matter-of-fact manner. The best possible emotional healing element is the overt expression of love. If the child wishes to talk about it, let him, but do not force him to discuss it. He *should* talk about it at some time, preferably to a loving parent. If not, to a good child therapist. Do not allow the incident to be emotionally suppressed. The pain involved with the incident should be resolved as soon after its occurrence as possible—but once again, without force, coercion, or persuasion.

What You Can Do to Prevent Homosexuality in Your Child

Ultimate answers are nice but impractical. They do not allow the human spirit its necessary freedom. What you will read in this section will not provide absolute protection from the insidious sin of homosexuality for your child. There is always the unknown quantity of his own choice of response to God, to himself, and to you as a loving parent. He has the right to reject God, himself, and you—outright. You must give him the freedom to act out that right. He will exercise it anyway, but if you give him the "space" to act it out, your relationship will be healthier and will stand a greater chance of remaining intact.

While I can give you no iron-clad promises, I can give you reasonable assurance that if you follow the following suggestions, you will greatly reduce the possibility of symptomatic homosexuality. Remember, homosexuality is *not a condition*. It is always a *symptom* of an environmentally produced *neurosis*. Obviously, the focus of prevention, then, is on providing an environment as free of neuroticism as possible. Before you write your family off as hopeless, please be assured that you are probably not much different from the family next door. However, given the homosexual incidence track record of the "normal" family, there is strong reason for genuine concern. So here are some "handles" to grasp. I wish you well:

Life-style

Living is a complicated adventure at best. I won't even mention what it can be at worst. What is it like in your home? Whatever it is like, you can count on this: Like a factory that produces a specific product, so will the "stamp" of your home be imprinted indelibly on the personality of your child. In short, how you cope with the complexities of living will in large measure be transmitted to your children. This includes how they feel about sex, sexuality, and the interaction between male and female.

1. *Reinforce gender definition by "role" interaction with your spouse.* This is especially important in the early years of childhood, and should be practiced consistently throughout their lives with you.

It is important here to make the point that by "role" I do not mean that one should divide household chores into male and female assignments. The work involved in maintaining a house and the functions of a family has no gender. It is no less masculine to wash a tubload of dirty diapers than it is to change a flat on the family car. It is no more feminine to select the curtains than it is to mow the lawn. I do not wish to argue the obvious, that some jobs lend themselves more to the physical constitution of one sex than to the other, but basically there is no such thing as "men's work," and "women's work." This is not the basis upon which productive sexual identification is formed.

By "role interaction" I mean that children should be given an overriding impression that males and females are to be maritally identified as a unit—a spontaneous, natural unit of happiness and warmth. They should see their mom and dad hugging, kissing, and touching each other. They must consistently observe the exchange of heterosexual love between their parents. How explicit this will be depends upon what is tasteful within that family's context: what constitutes an invasion of privacy and what does not. The point is that, by everyday life-style observation, children should be unmistakably aware that males were made for females, and vice versa.

2. *Parental reaction to heterosexual/homosexual stimuli will be noted and assimilated by children.* The most influential spokesman for the secular ethic within the American family constellation is the television set. Through its colorful eye is observed almost every conceivable form of human phenomena. Let's suppose a family is gathered around the tube comfortably watching a variety special. After the commercial, a lithe, seductively dressed female entertainer glides sensually across the screen to the rhythms of a throbbing melody.

Typical Christian family reaction:

Mother: "Oh, how awful!"

Father: "I should say! It's downright offensive how they allow trash like that on television at the family hour."

Son: "I have to go to the bathroom."

Daughter: "She has pretty hair."

Father whispers suspiciously to Mother, "Why do you think he wanted to go to the bathroom right now?"

Concerned expression on mother's face.

The point of this is not to argue the merits or dangers of television, but to illustrate how parental reaction to sexual stimuli can influence sexual identity formation in the mind of a child. Now here is another Christian family's reaction to the same program:

Daughter (giggles): "Mom, you'd better restrain Dad before he loses control."

Father (not taking his eyes off the TV, gives his wife a squeeze): "*You're* the one who turns me on, Sweetie!"

Mother: (Smiles with contented embarrassment.)

Son: (feeling subliminal satisfaction for the loving transference going on between his parents): "Quiet, you guys; I'm concentrating."

Perhaps neither family remotely resembles your own, but it is not hard to guess which family runs the greater risk as far as inadequate sexual formation in the development of their children is concerned.

3. *Cultivate a family life atmosphere of love, acceptance, and consideration.* This suggestion is directed more toward antineurosis than sexuality in particular. But it has been established that neurosis is the genesis for sexual as well as a host of other dysfunctional personality characteristics.

Regarding the sexual phenomenon in particular, it is crucial that a child feel comfortable in bringing a problem to a parent for consideration. Parents should be emotionally prepared to discuss *any* sexual question with loving objectivity and frankness. More will be said about discussion later, but it is clear that unless a child feels free to approach his parents with sexual questions without rejection, he certainly will refrain from doing so. Hot-headed flare-ups, cold indifference, religious pomposity, or assorted shades of disgust do nothing for the resolution of sexual conflicts. On the other hand, loving, sensitive parents, who are well oriented with respect to their own sexuality, have the least to fear from sexual aberration in their children.

Influence

The ability to cause someone to feel as you do about a given subject or value system is the measure of your influence with that person. Influence over another's behavior is usually tied to some sort of power-structure sanction. An employee will behave as his employer wishes, because if he does not, he will be damaged economically. His employer therefore has influence because of his economic power.

Influence over one's behavior is one thing. Influence over another's thought patterns and personality is quite something else. This can only be accomplished by a specific depth in a loving relationship. This may seem like a sweeping generalization, but I have never seen, nor can I think of, a single exception to it. Love on the feeling level is far and away the most powerful form of influence. For this reason we do those things that please God. I remain faithful to my wife not because I know it is wrong to commit adultery, but because I love my wife. She has the power of love to influence me to do things which please her.

Paradoxically, this power is inversely related to the ability to be influenced by the one over whom you possess a controlling influence. In other words, the reason I am so compelled to please God and my wife is that both God and my wife are likewise compelled to please me, because of their love for me. And in God's case, even more!

With respect to our children, our influence over them is absolutely crucial in their sexual and personality formation. If our influence is of the power-structure sanction variety (authoritarian, punitive, negatively biased, etc.), its overall and long-range effect, with respect to positively contributing to healthy personality, will be negligible. Its destructive potential is enormous.

However, if children are *genuinely feeling the love* of their parents, the influence factor is tremendous, and the value system of the parents will, eventually, generally be adopted. It should be noted that influence is the basis for all teaching. Without loving influence, teaching "concepts" will be inefficient. Without influence, parental image will not be enough. The "You will do this because I am your father and I told you to do it," is utterly absurd and ineffective without loving influence to fortify it. It may be absurd anyway.

Loving influence with children is achieved by: 1. Overt expressions of love: Saying "I love you" to them and meaning it; being physically affectionate with them; giving them individual and personalized attention; doing more than taking care of their general needs; disciplining them when they need it; being completely honest with them; telling them when you are angry with them instead of exploding at them; spending a few moments with them just before they fall asleep—in short, being to them what you would like God to be to you. 2. Apologizing to them when you have wronged them. Ask their forgiveness if it is called for. 3. By encouraging your child in his strengths and ideas. *Please do not throw cold water on your child's thoughts and ideas because of some stupid adult practicality.* You will do infinitely more damage to him than the consequences of his ideas. You can render your child no greater service than to help him prepare for the purpose which God intended for his life. You do not know what this purpose is. Your only clue is your child's deepest desires. One of the most beautiful experiences of life is to see how a child's gifts and talents usually develop along the lines of those things he most wants. 4. Be honest with yourself about your own strengths and limitations as a parent. This is called humility. With many people it is considered a weakness. With those who love you, it is a reason for respect.

Education

For me, sex education at the local school is a non-issue. For many well-meaning people, however, it poses a genuine threat. The thing about threats is that they are only threatening to those who are in danger of suffering from them. A threat to one's moral formation is meaningless if one's morals are secure. A loving family can neutralize any intrusion into its moral domain.

The primary source of sex education should indeed be the family. It is at least as important as the family altar—in my view, a hundred times more so. Almost all strong families have what is known as the family pow-wow. It is at this time that the family comes together for a discussion of household responsibilities, specific problems, better ways of relating, etc. Often it is an ongoing thing at mealtime. (Not recommended. Often bad for the digestion.)

How is a parent to go about this business of sex education? Should one keep quiet about it until a question is asked? Should one try to gear the information to the present participatory level of the child in question? In other words, should one feel free about explaining the use of condoms, sanitary napkins, and the vasectomy surgical procedure to a three-year-old? Are explicit graphics necessary? Is the family gathering a good time for such discussions? Should mothers talk to girls and fathers talk to boys? Whew!

Step number one: Responsible and spiritually sensitive parents should clear the air. Within the family context, talk about sex is not bad. Repeat: NOT BAD. Unless, of course, the family member doing the verbalizing speaks in vague, hard-to-understand concepts; unless he talks around the subject instead of directly about it; unless talk about sex cannot be expressed except by telling bad jokes.

Step number two: A good place to talk about sex is at the family conference. It is also good for a mother to talk to her daughter privately, or a father to his daughter privately. The same can be said for talking to sons. Mothers and fathers need not reserve specific data to be handled by one or the other. The information discussed should be wide-ranging and complete.

Step number three: As long as a child is old enough to understand what is being said, he is old enough to have it said to him. He may be three years old, thirteen, or twenty-three. As long as the concepts can be made clear so that they can be accurately grasped, the child is "old enough." Remember, we are not talking about something that is dirty or evil. We are talking about a God-given emotional and biological function. Fantasies like the stork, for instance, are counter productive.

Is propriety a factor? Certainly! But do not let propriety simply be an excuse for silence. It is too bad that society has taught us that talk about sex is really too private a matter, too delicate a subject to be discussed by "nonprofessionals." One need not wait for a child to broach the subject—indeed, a responsible parent must not wait. Discussion can be initiated by asking if your child has any questions about how they got here; about contraception; about lovemaking and its purpose; about spiritual standards and morals. If not, raise some questions and ask your child what he thinks about it.

Suppose your child comes up with questions about homosexuality? Or perhaps he begins to question his own sexuality? Deal with this in the same way that you deal with any value-system conflict. The philosophical basis for your answer will already be provided by your way of life. Provide corrective information. The degree to which there will be a positive response will be based on the mental imprint of the family's life-style and the measure of loving influence you have with your child.

Suppose your child is already homosexually traumatized? Do not waste time blaming yourself, your spouse, or someone or something else. Finding fault will not help your child. If anything will help him at this point, it will be a consistent love pattern. Do not treat your child as though he were "different." He has not changed. Only your awareness of his problem has changed. The odds are in favor of his needing professional attention.

The bottom line? As spiritually sensitive Christian parents we must provide a warm, loving environment, free from undue stress, in which our children may develop, and we must cultivate and possess a loving, empathetic influence to make effective corrections.

CHAPTER EIGHT

SHARING YOUR FAITH WITH A HOMOSEXUAL

I would like to make it clear that this is not a chapter on evangelizing the homosexual. If that is what you want, put a gold-plated fishhook in your lapel, stuff your pockets with copies of the four spiritual laws, slap a few "smile, God loves you," patches on your pants, and grab your Christian Worker's New Testament, and have at it.

But if you simply want to share yourself, your real self—and let others experience your faith by experiencing you; then maybe you will find this chapter relevant.

Dealing with Your Own Feelings: Prejudice and Panic

Mostly out of fear. That's where prejudice comes from. I grew up in Atlanta, Georgia. Although, for all practical purposes, I was raised by a black woman, I was also raised with prejudice. When I was a young man of fourteen or fifteen, I worked for my neighbor who was an electrical contractor. He taught me that if you only held on to one of the two wires in an electrical circuit, you would not be shocked. He also taught me that you always carried a gun when you drove through "cull'ed town." Whenever I went to visit Lizzie Mae, the woman who raised me, I was afraid. I was the only white among all those blacks. I used to wonder if they lived any differently than I did.

How do many heterosexuals feel about homosexuals today? Faggots, we call them. That's only one letter away from "*m*aggot"! "There is only one way," the man was saying as he softly whispered over the table, ". . . there is only one way to handle those people. And that is to take them all out and shoot them like dogs!" He was speaking about homosexuals. Nobody heard him but me and the man next to me. We were attending an international service club dinner.

So the first thing we heterosexuals should do is decide if we care enough to lay aside all of the prejudices and misinformation. If we really want to reach out and help, where must we begin? The answer to that question is, *with ourselves*. It is impossible to effectively give of ourselves unless we feel like doing so. It is impossible to love unless, within our hearts, we actually feel love.

May I then suggest that we entertain in our thoughts and prepare to take positive steps to befriend homosexuals? I do not mean we should join a program to help homosexuals. I do not mean "invite one over for dinner." Homosexuals do not wish to be patronized. We must learn to open our minds to them as human beings, and where appropriate, as fellow Christians. Allow yourself to think good thoughts of them, thoughts of compassion, thoughts of generous spirit.

Keep in your heart the spirit of Jesus toward the woman taken in adultery. You can love homosexuals and accept them without accepting or approving of their behavior. If in the course of everyday events you encounter someone who is homosexual, do not withdraw. Do not be afraid. Do not panic. Their symptom is not contagious. They do not foam at the mouth. They do not bite.

Meet the Problem: Inadequate Love

We said earlier that homosexuals are not primarily seeking sex—they are seeking to be loved. We also said that no amount of love will resolve the early childhood pain that provided for their homosexuality, with, of course, the singular exception of the love of God. This fact places believers in a unique position. They are the channels, allegedly, through which the love of God can flow. It is the love of a believer which has the amazing capacity of introducing a nonbeliever to the love of Christ.

What is it that makes a person feel loved by another? What quality of human chemistry forms the catalyst that transforms love felt into love communicated? In what behavior form does it result? The answer to these questions can best be understood by an examination of the crucifixion. The crucifixion of Jesus was prompted out of love for the likes of you and me. The behavior form that resulted from that love: *personal sacrifice.* The second point that should be noted is that while love always results in the behavior form of personal sacrifice, it *never demands* a behavior form in return. The only response that Jesus wanted from us was to be loved in turn. Love is not a performance. It is not a behavior form. But once the genesis of love occurs, personal sacrifice seems certain to follow.

In addition to nondemanding personal sacrifice, is the quality of *consistency.* The personal sacrifice of the crucifixion was in itself infinite. Still, those who have felt the love of Christ recognize that it exists in a continuum. It is always there. It is all-pervading, all-encompassing. There is nothing, absolutely nothing that can separate us from the love of Christ (Romans 8:30). *Not even homosexuality!*

The fourth and final quality of love communication is *determination.* It seems, in spiritual experience, that the Lord is always trying, always searching for a way to penetrate our resistances to being loved by him—for the inevitable result, once it is communicated and the circuit is established, is that his love will be returned by us. He is constantly adjusting the frequency of his transmission, seeking to reach our frequency of reception.

How is all this to be translated into relationships with homosexuals on the human level? Personal sacrifice? The first thing that should be sacrificed is our prejudices and demands. We should begin by placing our focus not upon their homosexuality, but upon their personhood and value as human beings. We do not try to get at their behavior by loving them. If we do that, we are being surreptitious and insincere. Jesus did not demand a certain behavior of us in return for his sacrifice. He demanded *relationship* instead. So we must be willing to say that we will love and accept the homosexual whether or not he gives up his homosexuality! For alcoholics, we have no problem in acknowledging this. For people who are destroying themselves with tobacco, we have no problem with it either. We should have no problem being a warm, loving, personable, accepting friend to the homosexual as well.

The truest test of the integrity of our love, however, will be its consistency, durability, and determination to make it felt. This will take countless and varied forms of communicative efforts. It will not stop. Ever. But its subliminal and conscious objective must never be behavior modification. All we can do is provide the opportunity for modification to occur. We must never demand it as a condition of our love.

What to Do When Propositioned

The chances are overwhelming that you won't be. In the face of a much enlarged activity among homosexuals, the chances have become even slimmer. The reason for this is the greater activity in itself. It is much easier for homosexuals to discover each other now than it ever was. The vast majority of them have no interest in possible physical confrontation or police involvement, especially when what they are looking for is so readily available in the gay bar or bathhouse. The homosexual church has provided a new social dimension for homosexual contact. So there is little need to accost strangers whose likelihood of being heterosexual is extremely high.

Still, there are those few who are interested in the thrill or the risk of approaching a "straight." For whatever kicks they get out of this sort of thing, it almost never works, unless the person approached is also interested in homosexual contact. But when their target is a straight, they are risk-taking and thrill-seeking. They know that they may be threatened or be beaten, or the police will be called. The usual response is a simple refusal. And that is the end of it.

If you are approached, refuse. It's that simple—unless there is specific felonious intent (in which case the complexion of the contact assumes a totally different demeanor). Homosexuals are like anybody else when rejected—they go their own way and deal with their feelings the best they can. *If the circumstances provide for it,* refuse in a manner which indicates rejection of sexual favors while leaving the way open to normal human interaction and friendship.

What to Do When You Learn
That a Loved One Is a Homosexual

Your fingers tremble as you hold the letter. You can't believe its contents. Your son in college has just "come out." He has admitted his homosexuality and tells you that he is living in a homosexual relationship with his roommate. Waves of nausea smack you in the stomach, you feel lightheaded and faint. His letter is hostile and declarative. He already knows how you will react and he has decided that he isn't going to let it bother him. He must be true, he asserts, to his feelings, to himself!

How you react may spell success or failure for any future relationship with your son or daughter. Indeed, how you react may tend to confirm him in his new lifestyle or, if handled with sensitivity, at least not contribute to it. If you approach it properly, you may help to bring him out of it. Some parents write their kids off. They write them off and consider them a non-son or non-daughter, and never want to see them again. Such parents are grossly irresponsible. They probably are the primary reason their child has opted for homosexuality.

If this sounds unwarranted, let me say that such parents have no doubt already established a pattern of reacting irrationally to their child's departures from their viewpoints. In such cases, the child would be lucky to escape without severe neurotic reaction. Neurotics breed neurotics if exposed to each other long enough.

Remain calm. Communicate your disappointment to your child as dispassionately as possible. Avoid hysterics, temper tantrums, and a "you can't do this to me" attitude. Along with your disappointment, communicate to him your love. It may be the first time he has felt it. Make sure that your feelings of love and acceptance come across to him. If he feels this, you will have gone a long way toward establishing channels of future positive relationship, should he, by whatever means, revert back to his heterosexuality.

Do Reject the Behavior

It may appear redundant to say this, but so many parents rationalize their children's behavior. They work it out emotionally so that their kids can do no wrong. Unless you have trained your mind to do it, it is hard to distinguish between the person and his behavior. It becomes easy to reevaluate homosexuality in the light of your love for your son. Or you may not want to face the fact that you might very well have been the cause of it . . .

In either case, we sometimes reason, "Well, maybe it isn't as bad as all that." You're right. It isn't. But when we allow ourselves the luxury of that emotional posture, we often jump from there to, "It's OK. It's really OK to be homosexual. He is just different, that's all. Like being left-handed."

Do not forget that your son's problem is correctable. He, of course, may not admit that it is a problem. There are millions of people in this country who are not well and not receiving treatment because they refuse to recognize it. Some of them will die. Their refusal to recognize it is, in the final analysis, the worst illness of all. Fortunately, homosexuality is not fatal. If you can do it without further alienation, encourage your child to receive treatment. It certainly can't hurt.

Relate to him spiritually. Let him know by the integrity of your own relationship with him, that God still loves him and accepts him. If he is a homosexual Christian, he may counter by telling you the same thing. Don't allow yourself to be intimidated. If he is argumentative, do not pursue it. This is why it is crucial to act out the love of God as well as talk about it.

Discover whether your community has a service to help homosexuals. If it does, call the group—even if it only serves to assist you in your relationship with your son. If it is a genuinely responsible program, its participants will be just as interested in helping you as your son.

NOTES

1. Troy Perry, *The Lord Is My Shepherd and He Knows I'm Gay* (Los Angeles: Nash Publishing, 1972), pp. 165–167.
2. Richard Green, Editor, *Human Sexuality* (Baltimore: The Williams & Wilkins Company, 1975), p. 74.
3. *Human Sexuality,* p. 80
4. James A. Michener, *Sports in America* (New York: Random House, 1976), p. 28.
5. Ed Kociela, *Los Angeles Herald Examiner,* 4/20/77, p. 6
6. Troy Perry, *The Lord Is My Shepherd, and He Knows I'm Gay* (Los Angeles: Nash Publishing, 1972), p. 3.
7. *Ibid.,* p. 5.
8. Arthur Janov, *The Primal Scream* (New York: G. P. Putnam & Sons, 1970), p. 308.
9. *Human Sexuality, New Directions in American Catholic Thought,* The Catholic Theological Society of America.
10. Arthur Janov, ed., *The Journal of Primal Therapy* Vol. IV, No. 1, Winter 1977, p. 63.
11. *Ibid., The Journal of Primal Therapy,* p. 56.
12. *Ibid., The Primal Scream,* p. 303.
13. Shere Hite, *The Hite Report* (New York: Macmillan Publishing Company, Inc., 1976), p. 413.
14. *Ibid., The Hite Report,* p. 416.
15. Perry, *The Lord Is My Shepherd,* pp. 150–153.
16. *Human Sexuality,* pp. 188, 191.
17. *The Journal of Primal Therapy* (Vol. III, No. 2), 1976.
18. Paul D. Morris, *Love Therapy* (Wheaton, Ill.: Tyndale House Publishers, 1974), pp. 99–106.

REFERENCES

Anonymous. "Can Primal Therapy Cure Homosexuality?" *The Journal of Primal Therapy*. 3 (2, 1976) 226–229.

Baars, Conrad W., *The Homosexual's Search for Happiness*. Chicago: Franciscan Herald Press, 1976.

Bakwin, Harry. "Deviant Gender-Role Behavior in Children: Relation to Homosexuality." *Pediatrics*. 41 (3, 1968), 620–629.

Beiber, Irving, et al. *Homosexuality: A Psychoanalytic Study*. New York: Basic Books, 1962.

Benjamin, H. *The Transsexual Phenomenon*. New York: Julian Press, 1966.

_____. "For the Practicing Physician: Suggestions and Guidelines for the Management of Transsexuals." *Transsexualism and Sex Reassignment*. (R. Green & J. Money, eds.) Baltimore; The Johns Hopkins Press, 1969.

Cappon, Daniel. *Toward an Understanding of Homosexuality*. Englewood Cliffs, N.J.: Prentice Hall, 1965.

Cavanagh, John R. *Counseling the Invert*. Milwaukee, Wis. Bruce Publishing Company, 1966.

Churchill, Wainwright. *Homosexual Behavior Among Males: A Cross-Cultural Species Investigation*. New York: Hawthorn Books, 1967.

_____. *The Gay Mystique: The Myth and Reality of Male Homosexuality*. New York: Stein and Day, 1967.

Coates, Stephen. "Homosexuality and the Rorschach Test." *British Journal of Medical Psychology*. 35 (2, 1962), 177–190.

Comfort, Alex, ed. *More Joy*. New York: Crown Publishers, 1973.

Cowell, R. *The Roberta Cowell Story*. New York: Lion Library, 1955.

Cross, Harold H. V. *The Cross Report on Perversion.* New York: Softcover Library, 1964.

Ellis, Albert. *Homosexuality: Its Causes and Cure.* New York: Lyle Stuart, 1965.

Fenichel, Otto. *The Psychoanalytic Theory of Neurosis.* New York: W. W. Norton, 1945.

Green, Richard, ed. *Human Sexuality, A Health Practitioner's Text.* Baltimore: Williams and Wilkins Co., 1975.

Hadfield, J. A. "The Cure of Homosexuality. *British Medical Journal* (5083, 1958), 1323–1326.

Hite, Shere. *The Hite Report, A Nationwide Study of Female Sexuality.* New York: Macmillan Publishing Co., 1976.

Hoffman, M. *The Gay World: Male Homosexuality and the Social Creation of Evil.* New York: Basic Books, 1968.

Holden, E. Michael. "A Quantitative Index of Pain Resolution in Primals with Discussion of Probable Relevant Biologic Mechanisms." *The Journal of Primal Therapy* 4 (1, 1977), 37–52.

———, Janov, Arthur. "The Birth of Neurosis: Transcript of a Lecture." *The Journal of Primal Therapy.* 4 (1, 1977), 53067.

———. "The Dialectic Unity of Healing and Suffering—The Primal Zone." *The Journal of Primal Therapy* 4 (1, 1977), 5–17.

Janov, Arthur. *The Primal Scream.* New York: G. P. Putnam's Sons, 1970.

Kinsey, Alfred C. "Homosexuality: A Criteria for a Hormonal Explanation of the Homosexual." *Journal of Clinical Endocrinology.* 1 (5, 1941), 424–428.

Kosnik, et al. *Human Sexuality, New Directions in Catholic Thought.* New York: Paulist Press, 1977.

Martin, D., Lyon, R. *Lesbian/Woman*. San Francisco: Glide Publications, 1972.

Masters, William H., Johnson, Virginia E. *Human Sexual Inadequacy*. Boston: Little, Brown and Company, 1970.

McCarthy, Barry W., et al. *Sexual Awareness*. San Francisco: Boyd and Fraser Publishing Co., 1975.

Money, John. *Sex Errors of the Body*. Baltimore: The Johns Hopkins Press, 1968.

Morris, Paul D. *Love Therapy*. Wheaton, Illinois: Tyndale House Publishers, Inc., 1974.

Ollendorff, Robert H. V. *The Juvenile Homosexual Experience and Its Effect on Adult Sexuality*. New York: Julian Press, 1966.

Perry, Troy. *The Lord Is My Shepherd and He Knows I'm Gay*. Los Angeles: Nash Publishing, 1972.

Philpott, Kent. *The Third Sex*. Plainfield, N.J.: Logos International, 1975.

Raley, Patricia, E. *Making Love*. New York: The Dial Press, 1976.

Roberta. *Gay Liberation*. Tustin, California: PTL Publications, 1975.

Rosen, Ismond, ed. *The Pathology and Treatment of Sexual Deviation: A Methodological Approach*. London: Oxford University Press, 1964.

Saghir, M., Robins, E. *Male and Female Homosexuality*. Baltimore: Williams and Wilkins, 1973.

Savitsch, Eugene de. *Homosexuality, Transvestism, and Change of Sex*. Springfield, Illinois: Charles C. Thomas, 1958.

Socarides, C. *The Overt Homosexual*. New York: Grune and Stratton, 1968.

Stapleton, Ruth Carter, *The Gift of Inner Healing*. Waco, Texas: Word Books, Publishers, 1976.

———. *The Experience of Inner Healing*. Waco, Texas: Word Books, Publishers, 1977.

Stoller, R. *Sex and Gender: On the Development of Masculinity and Femininity*. New York: Science House, 1968.

Wahl, Charles William, ed. *Sexual Problems: Diagnosis and Treatment in Medical Practice*. New York: Free Press, 1967.

Williams, Colin J., and Weinberg, Martin S. *Homosexuals and the Military*. New York: Harper and Row, 1971.

Young, William C., ed. *Sex and Internal Secretions*. 3rd. ed. 2 vols. Baltimore: Williams and Wilkins Company, 1961.